PUT YOUR BEST
FOOT FORWARD

Ministry for the Third Millennium
Edited by Lyle E. Schaller

PUT YOUR BEST FOOT FORWARD

How to Minister from Your Strength

JAMES O. ABRAHAMSON

ABINGDON PRESS / Nashville

PUT YOUR BEST FOOT FORWARD
How to Minister from Your Strength

This book is printed on recycled, acid-free paper.

Library of Congress Cataloging-in-Publication Data

Abrahamson, James O. 1944-
    Put your best foot forward : how to minister
from your strength / James O. Abrahamson.
        p.   cm.—(Ministry for the third millennium)
    ISBN 0-687-00491-8 (pbk. : alk. paper)
    1. Pastoral theology—United States.   2. Parishes—United States.
    BV4013.A37   1994
    250—dc20   94-9671
                                                                   CIP

Scripture quotations are from the New Revised Standard Version of the Bible, copyright © 1989 by the Division of Christian Education of the National Council of the Churches of Christ in the USA. Used by permission.

94 95 96 97 98 99 00 01 02 03—10 9 8 7 6 5 4 3 2 1

MANUFACTURED IN THE UNITED STATES OF AMERICA

*To the staff and elders of the Chapel Hill Bible Church
who encouraged the sabbatical project that eventually
led to this book*

CONTENTS

Contents

SECTION II: SIX STYLES EXAMINED

FOREWORD

What is a good church?

One answer to that question is, "It depends." The definition of a good church depends on the criteria used for evaluation. From the individual's perspective, a good church may be "one that speaks to my religious needs." For many parents, a good church is "one that interests and excites my children."

In the first volume in this series, Robert Randall began to answer that question by asking what people expect from church. He concluded that most people bring four yearnings to church. The first is a yearning to feel understood. The second is a yearning to understand what life is all about so they can order their lives. A third is a yearning to belong, to feel a sense of community. The fourth is a yearning for hope. (See Robert L. Randall, *What People Expect from Church*, Abingdon Press, 1992.)

The second volume in this series focused on that question from a different perspective and identified thirty recurring themes in outstanding center city churches of various sizes and types. Each one of the fourteen urban congregations described in that book merits the label "a good church." Together they illustrate the strength of North American Protestantism in the center city. Together they also illustrate the factors and forces that make for a good church. (See Lyle E. Schaller, ed., *Center City Churches*, Abingdon Press, 1993.)

This volume offers a different response to that question about a good church. It takes different kinds of good churches to reach different people. In this book, a veteran parish pastor identifies and affirms the legitimacy of six different types of good churches. There is no one answer to that question about the definition of a good church.

Instead of relying on the conventional twentieth-century categories for describing churches (position on the theological spectrum, community setting, age, denominational label, or size), this author comes up with a new conceptual framework. Jim Abrahamson contends that in the twenty-first century, the most significant line of demarcation that will distinguish one church from most others is the style of ministry. That is the most useful perspective for looking at the church in the third millennium.

The author goes on to identify, describe, and affirm six different styles of ministry. Each style has both strengths and weaknesses. These strengths and weaknesses are identified in an unusually precise, frank, and lucid manner.

Each one of the six styles is described by references to a New Testament church of that same style, by contrasting it with the other five styles, by identifying the central characteristics of that particular style, by references to contemporary examples of that style, and by a summary statement of strengths and concerns. The discussion of each of the six types concludes with a series of questions to help readers take inventory of their own congregation.

This book was written for many different audiences. Perhaps the most obvious is the call or pulpit nominating committee that is searching for a new pastor. Reading this book and answering the inventory questions following each chapter will enable the members of this ad hoc committee to be better equipped to identify and recommend the candidate who promises to be the ideal match.

A close second consists of members of the long-range planning committee. Their first assignment is to identify what the Lord is calling their congregation to be and to be doing five and ten years hence. Their second assignment is to define contemporary reality. The third step is to formulate the strategy for getting from "here" to "there." This book will help them identify the "here" of contemporary reality as well as elaborate on that vision of what the Lord is calling their congregation to be tomorrow. How do we translate that vision into operational terms? One way is to read this book.

A third audience consists of pastors who seek to understand more clearly and precisely (a) the congregation they are now serving, or (b) the "dream church" that they hope their present congregation will evolve into in the future, or (c) the congregation seeking a new pastor that has invited this minister to become a candidate to fill that vacancy. What are the questions a candidate should ask the members of that call committee? This book is filled with grist for that mill.

A fourth audience is the adult Sunday school class or book study group that seeks to gain a better understanding of the church in the twenty-first century.

A fifth audience consists of seminary students and doctor of ministry candidates who will find this book a unique conceptual framework for their studies.

A sixth, and possibly the second most appreciative audience, consists of denominational staff and parish consultants who will find this an exceptionally valuable tool for analysis of congregational life.

The most appreciative audience will consist of deeply committed, curious, future-oriented, and thoughtful Christians, both lay and clergy, who seek a clearer understanding of what worshiping communities may look like in the twenty-first century.

The most surprised audience may consist of those who place unity with diversity as their number one priority. They will be intrigued to discover the senior pastor of a large, nondenominational or independent church offering a clear, biblical, nonjudgmental, and persuasive call to unity while at the same time affirming the legitimacy of diversity in styles of ministry. That may be part of God's call to the churches in the third millennium!

LYLE E. SCHALLER
Net Results Resource Center
Naperville, Illinois

INTRODUCTION:
HOW TO READ THIS BOOK

Do all successful churches look alike? If our visit to twenty-five dynamic congregations is any indication, the answer is *no*.

Nearly every evangelical congregation recognizes the importance of *evangelism*, an English term translated from the ancient Greek word meaning "body count"! As congregations become more market-sensitive and creative, they will attract increasing numbers of people. But is this really the age of the mega-churches and metachurches only? Should all churches adopt a market-driven philosophy? Is numerical growth the only sign of success?

This book focuses attention on the churches of the twenty-first century. We believe that several different and legitimate styles of ministry offer something significant to those asking for a good church. As the new century approaches, style of ministry, not denominational label, is a primary consideration for many people.

In Search of the Successful Church

Few church leaders in pastoral ministry have a chance to visit and examine a large number of congregations over a short period of time. We had that opportunity when my family and I spent a three-month summer sabbatical on a cross-country tour to visit twenty-five of the most effective churches in the United States.

Our own ministry experience has been centered around one twenty-two-year pastorate in a university town, where our non-denominational church has grown from fifteen to fifteen hundred in worship, largely in isolation from any one model or tradition. Our church includes people from a wide variety of cultural and stylistic backgrounds. This diversity not only broadens our per-spectives, but also challenges our commitment to nurture a spirit of unity. Being in a liberal arts university environment where critical analysis is the major industry, our congregation had many questions and many opinions about how things were and should be. We are a church that does not lack educational training or cultural sensitivity. Nearly one-half of the official leaders in our church are men and women with earned doctorates in the sciences and humanities.

We began planning our trip a year before it took place. Sensing the need to see firsthand how other churches worked, we were encouraged by our church leaders to design a sabbatical project that would give us that exposure. We contacted a number of respected Christian leaders and asked each to give us the names of five congregations with unusually effective ministries. As our list grew, we noticed some congregations mentioned repeatedly.

We contacted the pastors of these congregations for the names of yet other model churches.

We targeted several congregations in specific metropolitan areas (Chicago, Los Angeles, Denver, Dallas, and others) in order to use our time more efficiently, but we also visited some out-of-the-way churches. Before starting our trip, we contacted each of the twenty-five churches and arranged to meet with the staff and lay leaders to observe services and to do whatever they thought would be most valuable to our study. We were grateful for the cooperation we received from large and small churches alike. During the trip we took notes, collected materials, and wrote summaries of each visit. After returning to North Carolina, we shared our observations with our church leaders. Then we started formulating some conclusions. We were guided by former exposure to church growth and leadership seminars, association with critical thinkers from various Christian traditions, and conditioning from our academic environment and other research.

We quickly observed that it takes different kinds of churches to reach different kinds of people. The congregations we saw varied from large megachurches such as Willow Creek Community Church in South Barrington, Illinois (fourteen thousand weekend attendees), to the relatively small churches (two hundred attendees) such as Trinity Church in Seattle, Washington. Some, such as Oak Cliff Bible Fellowship in Dallas, Texas, were predominantly black. Some were charismatic, like the Vineyard Fellowship in Anaheim, California. Others were denominational, like Covenant Presbyterian Church in West Lafayette, Indiana, while others were independent, like Elmbrook Church in Brookfield, Wisconsin. As we had hoped, most were quite different from our congregation in Chapel Hill, North Carolina.

We embarked on this journey with an open mind and genuine curiosity. Our desire was to learn from them first. We would critically evaluate what we observed and draw some conclusions later. Some of these conclusions were published in an article for *Leadership Journal* in the fall of 1991. This book is an expansion of that article.

Before we left our congregation in North Carolina, we expected to find a lot of similarities among the other congregations that we would visit. The differences among the churches we visited, however, were far greater than the similarities. We came back without a clear monolithic model of effective ministry. Instead, we found ourselves confronted with options and choices among the different styles of ministry.

Why This Book?

In this book we want to identify six specific styles of congregations within Christ's church in North America and assess the strengths and weaknesses of each. It is our observation that congregations spend too much time competing, criticizing, or comparing and not enough time affirming, supporting, and complementing other congregations that may differ in style.

Chapters 1 and 2 will introduce style as a distinguishing characteristic between congregations. In the first chapter we will introduce six styles of ministry: the reaching-up church, the reaching-down church, the reaching-in church, the reaching-out church, the reaching-back church, and the reaching-forward church. In the second chapter we will address the question: Should we have different styles or types of churches?

In chapters 3 through 8 we will look more carefully at each of the six styles mentioned above. We will explore both their strengths and their weaknesses. The book will draw some lessons from our journey in chapter 9.

Three benefits can be anticipated from reading this book. First, those who have a rather narrow perspective on how God's church can and should minister will be challenged to broaden our horizons. A second group of readers are those who feel insignificant because they are not like the megachurch across town. Perhaps this book will help them appreciate God's work in their midst even though it may be different elsewhere. A third group of readers may be confused as to where they fit in light of the many diverse styles of ministry in Christ's church. For them this book can expand their appreciation for six styles within Christ's church and help them find their own unique identity.

We hope that all groups not only will gain a deeper understanding of the legitimate diversity among Christian churches, but also will learn to appreciate and celebrate their own strengths in ministry. As we prepare to enter the twenty-first century, this book is a call to appreciate our differences and provide affirmation through a sober assessment of these differences. The information in this book reflects perceptions of this author that have been verified through the feedback of a number of professional church watchers. We further believe that a growing number of people in our culture are coming to share these same perceptions of the church. Consumers' perceptions often lead to expectations that in turn energize the forces that shape the face of the church in the future.

SECTION I

Styles Are In

1.

Body Language

Your Church's Ministry Style Shapes Its Image.

What Kind of Church Do You Attend?

Two ministers from different denominations were the best of friends, but often disagreed on religious issues. One day they had been arguing more than usual on a theological point, when one of them said: "That's all right. We'll just agree to disagree. The thing that counts is that we're both doing the Lord's work—you in your way, and I in His."

The North American church is remarkably diverse, with each sect believing that it is in the center of God's will. While being careful to avoid one state-sponsored church, Americans have seen the proliferation of over one thousand sects and denominational groups. Individuals can choose from a literal smorgasbord of religious institutions in America. How does one sort out the seemingly endless options? For many the choice is simply a matter of following the tradition of their parents. If they grew up Methodist, they remain Methodist. However, many people are making other choices about where they will worship, choices that break from the old patterns.

Traditionally, the Protestant church has been divided or categorized along one of a number of lines, the most common category being *denominational affiliation*—that is, Baptist, United Methodist, Presbyterian, Lutheran, and so on. This distinction is still very important to many people. However, as individuals are beginning to feel comfortable jumping from one denominational nest to another, we are left with the impression that denominational loyalty is a thing of the past. As one leader shared with us, "In our denomination we are aware of a whole new generation of churchgoers who couldn't care less about continuing in the choice of their parents. Our appeals for denominational loyalty are ignored as an irritation." This tendency is consistent with the trend in the larger culture to move from community, idealism, and corporate welfare to individualism, pragmatism, and individual autonomy.

A second distinction used to classify differences among churches arose as a result of the modernist/fundamentalist controversies of the nineteenth century. The terms *liberal* and *conservative* became meaningful labels for congregations depending on how they chose to relate to the modern world, especially historical-critical scholarship. For some this issue still distinguishes one congregation from another, but for many people in our day the interest has moved away from biblical theology to practical theology. Churchgoers are seeking less emphasis on theological precision and more on practical help in applying biblical truth to life—work, marriage, child rearing, emotional health, and the like.

In the sixties and seventies a third distinction of *charismatic* and *non-charismatic* had meaning. Today this distinction seems less important. The two extremes of *charismania* (an obsessive preoccupation with the sign gifts of tongues and healing) and *charisphobia* (a paranoid fear of emotionally driven spirituality) are fading.

A fourth way in which churches have been categorized is size. A conspicuous gap is growing between large and small congregations. Two-thirds of all congregations in America have an average Sunday attendance of 120 or less. However, most of us are not going to a small church on Sunday. While the number of metropolitan megachurches is small, these congregations get much attention because they serve so many people. Twenty percent of all congregations in the United States account for over one-half of all churchgoers on a typical weekend. In an age of superstores, megamalls, and extensive mobility we are seeing full-service, seven-day-a-week churches that cater to and reflect the spectator/consumer culture.

In addition to the traditional ways of distinguishing among various congregations (denomination, liberal/conservative, charismatic/non-charismatic, and size), we want to suggest that style of ministry will increasingly be the issue in many people's minds. It is not uncommon today to hear people speak of churches with labels like megachurches and metachurches, relational churches, Bible-teaching churches, and so forth. Type or style of ministry is becoming as important as denominational labels in the minds of a growing number of people. This new sensitivity to style suggests a whole new set of categories as we survey the diversity among Christian congregations.

What Is Your Style?

Most of the churches we visited offered substantial amenities on several fronts while being outstanding in at least one area. However, that area of excellence varied from congregation to congregation. For example, a small congregation just outside Chicago has excellent biblical preaching that helps many people. However, this church does not have the outreach focus of another congregation in the same area. Our observation is that most congregations have one distinct style that forms the core of their reputation in the community. That style can be centered in teaching, worship, outreach, relationships, tradition, social action, or something else. These differences in style do not reflect deficits in character so much as uniqueness in direction of ministry.

Reaching in One Primary Direction

It is difficult to do justice to the great diversity of styles, but let us suggest some broad-style categories that will help distinguish among the churches we have visited. Because our visits were relatively short and not as thorough as we would have liked, we run the risk of being too intuitive in our assessments. We sense that six styles can be distinguished.

If asked to describe themselves in terms of these style categories, most of the congregations would say they are striving for balance. A congregation may fear that by acknowledging one area of strength, they necessarily are implying other areas of weakness or dysfunction. In reality, several areas in a congregation may be functioning in a healthy way, but one area sets the style or the image of the church. We should not hesitate to identify a church's strongest asset as its style.

The six styles of churches in this book represent six different directions in which a congregation can move, reach, or look as it develops its ministry emphasis.

First, we recognize the *reaching-up church*. This worship-centered congregation often has a charismatic flavor, but not always. It sees the worship experience as the hub around which everything else revolves. People come to this church first and foremost to sense the presence and glory of God.

The second type of church we call the *reaching-down church*. This congregation emphasizes the ministry of the Word of God coming from on high to the people and is noted for its biblical teaching. The Word of God is unfolded before people who come to learn. Everything else in the Sunday service seems like "pregame warmup" to the sermon, which is more teaching than preaching.

Third, we have the *reaching-in church*. This congregation emphasizes relationships. It majors on fellowship and relational dynamics and provides a safe environment where members can honestly share life's joys and sorrows. People are challenged to look inside themselves and to cultivate a rich, social/spiritual infrastructure through small groups.

The fourth style of church we designate as the *reaching-out church*. These market-driven, outreach-centered congregations often become megachurches and receive unusual publicity for their innovative and sometimes controversial strategies to reach their communities. (Recently the church growth movement has fueled interest in this style of ministry with scores of books on the demographic and sociological dynamics of our culture and how to reach it.)

The fifth style, the *reaching-back church,* is concerned about holding fast to the traditions of the historical roots of its faith. This group is often fiercely denominational and stoutheartedly confessional. Often these congregations are convinced that change is more a threat or accommodation to culture than a need.

Sixth is the *reaching-forward church*. These congregations are concerned about and committed to changing society as they focus attention on national and international affairs. These churches may be politically conservative like Liberty Baptist in Lynchburg, Virginia, or progressive, like The Church of the Savior in Washington, D.C.; but each is striving to influence public policy in the direction of distinctly Christian values of peace, justice, human rights, and so forth.

The Style Sphere

We might summarize the various styles of ministry with a diagram. Picture the fullness of Christ as a sphere with the cross of Christ at the core. Six radiating arms extend from the core to support the surface of the sphere. Each of these arms represents one aspect of ministry, that is, a style or an emphasis. Each aspect of ministry radiates from a central unifying source, the cross of Christ, which is the symbol of Jesus' substitutionary sacrifice. While healthy congregations will display life in each of the six areas represented by the radiating arms in the diagram, at least one area will be outstanding and mark a congregation's style.

What Factors Determine Your Style?

In our observation, at least five factors shape a congregation's style: the ministry style of the founding pastor or group, the present leadership, the culture in which the congregation ministers, the gifts of the people in the congregation, and the history of the congregation.

The *ministry style of the founding pastor* can cast a long shadow over a church. This fact is especially true if the pastor has had a powerful and effective ministry in one area. For example, the ministry of S. Lewis Johnson at Believers' Chapel in Dallas, Texas, set a pace in the direction of expository Bible teaching that marked that congregation far beyond the pastor's tenure there. Those who followed Dr. Johnson were expected to perpetuate this strong emphasis on Bible teaching.

The *present leadership*, especially if powerful and effective, can play a role in refining the style of a congregation. An outstanding example is seen in the ministry of Jim Tozer at Covenant Presbyterian in West Lafayette, Indiana. After several years at Covenant, Tozer's personal, spiritual revival resulted in the whole congregation's move from a traditional style to a more active, relational style. The congregation is now noted for its small-group ministry. Those who were familiar with this congregation before and after Tozer's personal transformation told us that the congregation represented two different styles of churches. One congregation was dead and holding on to little but tradition; the other was alive and reaching out and in with vision and purpose.

The *setting or culture in which a congregation ministers* plays an important role in its style. For example, a congregation in a university town might have a teaching ministry, whereas a congregation in a rural southern culture may be more relational and community-centered. A church in a hostile inner city may be more evangelistic, while a church in a heavily Christianized small town may be more worship-centered.

The *strengths of the members* can play a big part in shaping a congregation's style. For example, a congregation built upon the foundation of families with a strong commitment to close relationships is probably going to be a relational or inward-looking church. To the extent that the people are the dominant influence in the church, their contribution of strength and style will shape that congregation.

The *history of a congregation*, especially in a period of crisis, can play a major role in shaping its style. Some congregations have experienced rather dramatic changes in ministry style as the result of a church split or spiritual revival. Where the charismatic movement has had an impact, often an upward shift influences the church to become more worship-centered.

Some denominations carry with them a definite style preference. For example, the Assemblies of God are known for their worship, and the Southern Baptists for their outreach.

Traditional ways of differentiating between congregations

- Denominational affiliation
- Conservative vs. liberal
- Charismatic vs. non-charismatic
- Large vs. small

A new way of differentiating among congregations

- **Style of ministry**

  Reaching up—worship
  Reaching down—teaching
  Reaching in—relational
  Reaching out—market-driven
  Reaching back—traditional
  Reaching forward—social action

Factors that determine style

- The founding pastor
- The present pastor
- The environment
- The gifts of the people
- The history of the church

2.

IT TAKES ALL KINDS

CHURCHES CAN BE UNITED IN SPIRIT YET DIVERSE IN STYLE.

Different Strokes for Different Folks

Is diversity of style a legitimate and desirable characteristic for Christ's church? Should we all expect to look alike if we follow the same Lord?

A young visitor to a liturgical church service in Minnesota raises her hands during a worship service and shouts out loud, "Praise the Lord!" The shocked congregation responds with glares of astonishment. A few minutes later, not able to contain herself, she shouts again, "Praise the Lord!" This time, a mother sitting behind her taps her on the shoulder and sternly corrects her. "We don't 'praise the Lord' in this church." Her son, sitting next to her, hears the advice and corrects his mother with, "Oh, yes, we do, Mom. It's on page seventeen."

Someone once said, "There are two types of people in the world, those who are like us and those who should be like us." What do the distinct characteristics in our worship or ministry styles mean? Are those who differ from our particular style displaying signs of some theological or spiritual pathology?

In this chapter we want to affirm the diversity of expressions among Christ's congregations. We believe that the differences among churches may not be just the fruit of human depravity or cultural happenstance, but may be a natural and positive part of God's plan. Diversity is certainly a part of God's design in nature, and we see it also in individuals as well as in cultures. Should we not expect to see it in congregations as well? Diversity in style and emphasis need not threaten unity of spirit, but should rather deepen our capacity to appreciate the fullness of Christ. Diversity need not threaten faithfulness and fruitfulness, but should encourage and enhance them. Diversity should not threaten us if we follow Christ.

Longings and Styles

If the church of Jesus Christ is going to bear witness to the twenty-first century, it must speak in known tongues to felt needs with spiritual insight. It must provide meaningful relational, learning, worshiping, serving, remembering, and social-change experiences. As our world becomes more technological, we long for *contact with transcendence* and spiritual mystery. In the face of an information explosion, we long for *insight and understanding*. As we are isolated from one another by space and machines, we hunger for *intimacy in relationships*. As we see ministry reserved for professionals, we need to know how we can be *significant*. In the face of rapid and constant change, we long for something to *remain the same*. As society becomes more decadent and unjust, we long for a *social utopia* of peace and justice.

We observe that any individual congregation tends to be more sensitive to at least one of these felt needs than to others. A congregation's sensitivity will set it up to speak more powerfully and directly to certain areas of human need than to others. This emphasis tends to set the style of a church's ministry.

Acts 2:42-47 provides an interesting reference to at least six functions of the church, functions that loosely parallel types of style highlighted in this book. The Christians in Jerusalem "devoted themselves to the apostles' teaching" (v. 42—reaching down); "and fellowship" (v. 42—reaching in); "to the breaking of bread" (v. 42—reaching back); "awe came upon everyone" (v. 43—reaching up); "day by day the Lord added to their number those who were being saved" (v. 47—reaching out); and "having the goodwill of all the people" (v. 47—reaching forward). Again, it must be stated that a healthy congregation is going to manifest each of these functions, but not necessarily with the same degree of skill or effect in each area.

Christ's Church Is Multifaceted

Is the purpose of the church to be centered in outreach, relationships, worship, education, service, tradition, or social change? Two assumptions often go unchallenged when any of us respond to this question.

First, we tend to assume that our particular style or emphasis is right and that those with different styles are in need of correction. If we are a worship-centered church and do that well, we may assume that worship is the measure of a healthy, good church. If we are teaching-oriented, we probably use teaching to measure the health of every congregation. We measure others against our strengths.

The second assumption that North American, evangelical, Protestant churches often make is that the evangelistic call of the "great commission" (Matt. 28:19-20) is the heart of the church's purpose. But are we reading Matthew 28 correctly? Too often this mandate is misunderstood to center on evangelization of the lost. It is, in fact, more appropriately centered on the bringing of all people to spiritual *maturity* (John 21:15-17; Eph. 4:11-24). Evangelism is but the first step in the process of leading people to grow to maturity.

It is significant, if not compelling, to look at the emphasis in the apostles' teachings to the early church as recorded in the epistles. Little attention is given to evangelism. In Paul's version of "the great commission" (Eph. 4:11-24), most of the attention is given to the spiritual and moral infrastructure of the Christian community. In other words, the letters are written to Christians regarding their relationships to other Christians.

Please do not misunderstand this clarification to mean that world outreach is not important to God's heart and the church's purpose. Reaching the spiritually lost is very important. However, we should challenge the notion that the *only* real business of the church is reaching the lost world with the gospel and also the corollary assumption that the best sign of success is numerical growth or number of baptisms. The market-driven model of ministry has its place, but it is not the only way to do ministry.

Paul's letter to the Ephesians suggests that the church's purpose is more appropriately understood as a balanced and multifaceted *response to Christ*—a response that is not unlike the body responding to the head (Eph. 4:11-16), the bride responding to the bridegroom (Eph. 5:22-33), and the building relating to the cornerstone (Eph. 2:19-22). This response to Christ involves a number of things—namely worshiping, learning, serving, relating, evangelizing, remembering, and affecting society.

If we were going to articulate the purpose of the church in one sentence, it might read like this: *The purpose of the church is to glorify God by responding to the Lord Jesus Christ through exalting him as Creator, Redeemer, and Lord; educating his people; edifying (discipling) his body the church; evangelizing his world; encompassing the traditions of the faith; and enriching the broader culture.* While all congregations should ideally be effective in each of these areas, most will be stronger in one area than in all the others. Churches are usually characterized by their unique strength. In our community, for example, one church prides itself in its spirit of worship, while another sees itself as focused on outreach into the community.

ACTS 2	STYLES OF CHURCH MINISTRY	LONGINGS OF MODERN PERSONS	PURPOSES OF CHRIST'S CHURCH
V. 43 "A sense of awe"	REACHING **UP**	**TRANSCENDENCE** (Worship) in the face of "technology"	**EXALT** Christ as Creator, Redeemer, Lord
V. 42 "the teaching of the Apostles"	REACHING **DOWN**	**INSIGHT** (teaching) in the face of "information"	**EDUCATE** Christ's people
V. 42 "fellowship"	REACHING **IN**	**INTIMACY** (relationships) in the face of "isolation"	**EDIFY** Christ's church
V. 47 "adding to their number daily"	REACHING **OUT**	**DIRECTION** (tradition) in the face of "professionalism"	**EVANGELIZE** Christ's world
V. 42 "breaking of bread"	REACHING **BACK**	**STABILITY** (tradition) in the face of "temporality"	**ENCOMPASS** the past
V. 47 "having favor with all the people"	REACHING **FORWARD**	**UTOPIA** (ideal society) in the face of "injustice"	**ENRICH** the culture

Differences Are Not Deficits

Many profound differences that we encounter when relating to other people cannot be ascribed to differences in moral or emotional maturity, and are not a matter of random chance. Patterns, when understood, give us insight into how and why we are different. For example, some people have an introverted posture toward life (gathering energy from inner reflection), while others are extroverted (gathering energy from their external environment). The extroverted person in an audience tends to give a speaker lots of feedback through eye contact, body language, and facial expressions. The introverted person appears to be totally uninvolved, but in reality may be more engaged than the extrovert.

It would be a mistake to assume that the introverted person is socially damaged, spiritually apathetic, or culturally retarded just because he or she is not as outwardly responsive. An introverted person may appear to be a "party pooper," while in reality he or she may be pooped by the party. Large crowds and small talk wear introverts out, but this response does not mean that they are inferior to extroverts. The important point to remember is that a particular style is not good or bad; it is just distinct and different. We think that this principle should be applied to congregations as well.

Put Your Best Foot Forward, but Don't Kick Your Neighbor

Growing up in a traditional Lutheran congregation in the Midwest, we acquired a perception of what constituted a worship service. The order of the service, like the ministry agenda of the congregation, was fixed and has changed very little over the years. We are currently pastoring in a nondenominational congregation that draws many university students. Our worship is relatively informal, and our order of service changes often. Those who come to our Sunday morning services are prepared to be surprised. They may find a drama skit, open congregational sharing, African music, or any one of a number of other unique features. Knowing that our congregation consists of people with different tastes and styles, we seek to offer an opportunity for varied participation and involvement.

Differences in emphasis and style are apparent in Anglican, Baptist, or charismatic fellowships. These differences are sometimes a reflection of a cultural or theological emphasis, that is, in the broader scope of things, neither right nor wrong.

To be sure, theological differences affecting style are sometimes critical to our faithfulness to the gospel, but we must be careful that we not split hairs and major on minors in defining the "true church." We can too easily make dogmatic theological assertions as to why we adopt one way of doing things over another when actually the real factors that distinguish us are cultural or stylistic preferences having little to do with theology. For example, the evangelical theology shared by John McArthur's Grace Church in California and Bill Hybel's Willow Creek Church in Illinois is substantially the same, but the philosophy of ministry is quite different. Grace Church follows a more conservative cultural style, while Willow Creek is willing to "color outside the traditional lines" in speaking to its culture.

In reading the New Testament, it is hard not to sense that God is much more concerned about our unity of Spirit than about our ability to bring everyone in line with our ministry style, especially when our cultural traditions have the effect of excluding some of those embraced by Christ.

This point came home to us in a dramatic way while participating in an evangelical congregation in the late 1960s. The qualifications for membership and leadership in this particular congregation were noticeably exclusive. None of the Reformers (because of their views on eschatology), few, if any, of the church fathers (because of their views on water baptism), and not even the apostle Paul (because he spoke in tongues) could have served in positions of leadership in this church. In some cases they could not have even been members because of detailed doctrinal or social distinctions. As a matter of fact, Jesus himself would have been excluded from leadership in this church because he drank wine and was not married. Upon seeing such exclusionary requirements, we wondered how such a congregation could still call itself Christian. Sometimes our arbitrary distinctions are not so much a sign of our faithfulness to the truth, keeping us from apostasy, as a tool used by the enemy, keeping us from spiritual growth by separating us from one another, or dividing the body of Christ. The fullness of Christ, which Satan would thwart, involves diversity among God's people.

The First-Century Churches Were Diverse

A healthy respect for diversity seems to be on Paul's mind in Romans 12:3-8 when he speaks of "gifts that differ." The fact that we see things through different lenses and relate to the kingdom in different ways does not at all imply that we are not united. Paul's concern in Romans 12 is to show that even when we are "living sacrifices" (Rom. 12:1), we still have "gifts that differ" (Rom. 12:8). That is to say, our sharing in the death of Christ on the cross does not nullify our distinctive strengths. We do not become clones.

As churches look at their own style of ministry, do they see their emphasis as a blessing or an embarrassment? Sometimes it seems we feel compelled to live up to a stereotype that is not our calling. For example, we have heard more than one person declare categorically that 50 percent of our church budget should be devoted to foreign missions or other ministries outside the church family. When we ask them why, they say, "That is the mark of a mature church." A big mission budget may be a sign of maturity for another congregation, but not necessarily for our congregation; our role may be to work with international students at the local university. Working with local international students while reflecting a commitment to missions does not require a large budget outlay.

When we look at the congregations described in the New Testament, we see diversity in matters of ministry emphasis and strength. The church at Corinth was noted not only for its carnality, but also for its giftedness in areas of worship and charismatic signs (1 Cor. 1:7). The church at Thessalonica was noted for its outreach (1 Thess. 1:8). The Berean Jews who formed a church were noted for their careful scrutiny of scripture (Acts 17:11). Even today, when the name Berea is used, it suggests a careful examination of the Bible.

We see a diversity also in the way in which the apostle Paul ministered to different communities. In Athens, he spoke as a philosopher (Acts 17:16-34) and in Corinth as a simple man (1 Cor. 2:1-5). Should we not respect this same kind of diversity in our day? The small country church, the congregation near a university campus, the market-driven megachurch, and the traditional denominational congregation each has characteristic strengths and weaknesses that are not necessarily a reflection of any kind of spiritual pecking order; these churches are simply different.

Faithfulness and Flexibility

While style can be a helpful tool in understanding diversity among congregations, it must be refined with some other distinctions. For example, many differences exist within each of our style categories. Not all worship-centered or teaching-centered congregations look alike.

One of the most important distinctions among churches within a particular style category has to do with the way they relate to modern culture and to the historic tenets of the faith. Their flexibility within their culture and their faithfulness to the Christian message are characteristics that reflect their spiritual health, as well as shape their style.

To meet the challenge of the twenty-first century, our churches must be both faithful and flexible. Faithfulness to the timeless truth of Christianity requires a radical sensitivity to the language and spirit of historic Christianity. Flexibility to the culture in which we minister likewise requires a sensitivity to the language and spirit of our age.

In the face of the challenge of a dynamic culture, churches tend to follow one of four responses: neither faithful nor flexible, flexible but not faithful, faithful but not flexible, and flexibly faithful. The following chart shows us how these responses further define a reaching-down or teaching-centered church.

	NEITHER FLEXIBLE NOR FAITHFUL	FAITHFUL BUT NOT FLEXIBLE	FLEXIBLE BUT NOT FAITHFUL	FLEXIBLE FAITHFULNESS
REACHING UP				
REACHING DOWN	Theologically and culturally irrelevant	Theologically orthodox but culturally out of touch	Theologically confused but culturally relevant	Theologically orthodox and culturally relevant
REACHING IN				
REACHING OUT				
REACHING BACK				
REACHING FORWARD				

The second way in which we can distinguish between congregations within a particular style is by giving attention to temperament characteristics.

Temperaments Within Each Style

It is apparent to most observers that both Charles Swindoll and John McArthur have teaching-centered ministries. However, they and their congregations are different enough in style to warrant some kind of special categorization. How can we distinguish between churches within one of the six styles when they display significant differences while still reaching in the same basic direction? Temperament theory may be a key.

The Greek philosopher Hippocrates identified four basic temperament types: melancholic, sanguine, phlegmatic, and choleric. David W. Keirsey, using the Myers-Briggs Type Indicator, has offered the most recent and popular expression of these four ways of relating to life. He refers to the *SJ* (*S*ensing/*J*udging) type as those who give attention to details and have a need for system and order. This type tends to preserve traditions and emphasize duty and responsibility by following the rules. He refers to the *SP* (*S*ensing/*P*erceiving) type as those who give attention to details but value freedom to adapt to changing situations. This type tends to prefer free expression and action-oriented service. People of this type tend to be less structured and more independent. The third temperament type is the *NT* (*IN*tuitive/*T*hinking) type in Keirsey's system. The people of this type look at life as a succession of new problems to be solved or understood. They tend to be focused on theoretical truth and strive for the understanding of how truth is integrated into all of life. The fourth and last temperament type Keirsey identified as the *NF* (*IN*tuitive/*F*eeling) type. This type of individual tends to place high value and high expectations on relationships between people.

Each of these four types can be a helpful tool in characterizing any organization, including a Christian congregation. The personality type of key leaders, especially the senior pastor, can shape the personality type of a whole ministry.

If we were to imagine each of these four temperaments finding expression within each of the six styles of ministry, we would have a model that more completely distinguishes one congregation from another within the same style. The following chart can help us understand how these styles and temperaments interact.

	LAW & ORDER "RULES"	ACTION "FREEDOM"	REASON "TRUTH"	IDEALISM "CARING"
WORSHIPING REACHING **UP**	Strong controls from leadership	Loose structure and room for free expression	Emphasis on content more than affective expression	Care and respect for individual expression
TEACHING REACHING **DOWN**	Prescribed beliefs and behaviors	Challenge to action and service with freedom to be creative	Understand-ing principles and theories	Emphasis on personal experiences and TLC
RELATING REACHING **IN**	Set structures for ministering to people	Encourage-ment to spontaneous service to others	Emphasis on understanding people's problems	Attention given to people as individuals
EVANGELIZING REACHING **OUT**	Set procedures for doing evangelism	Freedom to be creative and minister spontaneously	Attention given to rationale for each ministry	Friendship evangelism through relationships
PERSERVING REACHING **BACK**	Set liturgy or traditions that have not changed	Serving is active but in traditional ways	Careful philosophical attachment to the past	Romantic attachment to the past
SOCIAL CHANGE REACHING **FORWARD**	Structured approach to changing society	Dynamic activist approach to change	Careful, rational debate of issues	Radical social modeling with emphasis on individuals

SECTION II

Six Styles Examined

3.

THE REACHING-UP (WORSHIP-CENTERED) CHURCH

EXPERIENCING THE PRESENCE OF GOD

It was A. W. Tozer who reminded us that we are here to be worshipers first and workers only second. We take a convert and immediately make a worker out of that person. God never meant it to be so. God meant that a convert should learn to be a worshiper, and after that he or she can learn to be a worker. The work done by a worshiper will have eternity in it. A logical first stop in our discussion of ministry styles is the worship-centered church.

The reaching-up churches, centering ministry around worship and prayer, seem to come in two distinct types: charismatic and liturgical. Since most of the liturgical churches seem to fit also in the reaching-back church to be discussed in chapter 7, our comments here will center on the charismatically oriented congregations that we have observed.

Corinth

Corinth was the site of one of the most exciting Christian congregations in the first century. It is a shame that the congregation at Corinth is remembered primarily for its excesses—immorality, selfishness, pride, and preoccupation with temporal blessings. The Corinthian Christians should also be remembered for their strong sense of the powerful immanence of God's Spirit.

If for a moment we can refocus our attention on the attractive assets that the Corinthian church offered, we can get a feeling for the magnetic pull that a number of modern day worship-centered congregations have on people of all socioeconomic classes. In a culture that has systematically explained away much of the awe, mystery, and supernatural power of the living God, many of us still hunger for tangible expressions of God's presence in this life. We describe these churches as "reaching up" because they are seeking an encounter with the living God in their worship.

Many Christians believe that you can tell a lot about a church by just observing its people in worship. Are the worshipers just maintaining a tradition, soothing their conscience, being entertained, or are they in awe of the living God?

Characteristics

The charismatic, worship-centered church is unique in that *praise, prayer, and worship are at the center of its life.* Nearly every meeting will include praise and worship. A business meeting, Bible study, or small group will begin with praise and worship. An evangelistic outreach may begin, or more likely end, with praise and worship.

When you ask the leaders of a worship-centered congregation to describe the characteristics of a healthy or mature church, they will put the quality of praise and worship near the top of the list.

Praise and worship are seen as the goal of ministry and the primary reason for the church's existence. It is a mistake to conclude that other functions like teaching, outreach, fellowship, and so forth are not present or not viewed as vital in a worship-centered church. They are often very strong, but the central feature will be praise and worship. When people who are drawn to such a church are asked why they go to this church and not another, they will likely mention the quality of the worship.

Examples

The Vineyard Fellowship in Anaheim, California, is a model of the charismatic congregation that emphasizes worship and the power of prayer. We found the morning service to be like many, large charismatic gatherings—worshipful, spontaneous, lively, but it was what happened after the service that impressed us most. Several hundred people stayed around for prayer.

The sermon had little or nothing to do with intercession or healing. No one from up front invited people to stay, but my wife and I decided to request prayer for some unresolved personal challenges in our lives.

A rather unassuming, middle-aged counselor listened to our brief request and then asked if we had a good, spiritual support group back in North Carolina. We assured him that we did, and then he said that in a few moments we would understand why that was so important. He laid his hands on us and quietly prayed—in English and then in tongues.

Shortly after this dramatic experience my wife began to experience a new freedom from inner obsessions. The next several weeks were emotionally tumultuous for her as she began to overcome the pain of her past. Today my wife is amazed that through the power of prayer after that service, a healing was begun that four years of intense counseling had not been able to accomplish.

Another such congregation we visited is Applegate Christian Fellowship near Medford, Oregon. We met the pastor Jon Courson at a leadership forum a year before our trip and were immediately drawn to him. We could not wait to visit his congregation. His charisma and giftedness in so many areas (teaching, leading worship, personal relations) help explain why Applegate Christian Fellowship in a rural county draws thirty-five hundred people on Sunday.

Applegate has three types of meetings during the week. Wednesday night is ninety minutes of expository Bible teaching. Sunday morning is praise and worship with an uplifting message, which exhorts people to apply the lessons taught on Wednesday night. The Sunday evening service centers around the Lord's Table and prayer for freedom from emotional, physical, and spiritual bondage. As people feel led (during any part of that service), they go forward to receive the bread and cup. There is no sermon, just people bringing their burdens to God's Table in a spirit of worship. Pastor Courson told us that when people come to him for counseling, he first sends them to the Sunday evening service. After going to the service, people often do not need counseling.

Strengths

1. Personal boldness and confidence in ministry characterize many of these churches. Charismatic, worship-centered churches possess great strengths. In the congregations that we visited evangelism was effective; they attracted and saw many converted from unbelief. These conversions were often dramatic testimonies to God's power and mercy. We talked to one young man who was delivered from substance abuse (drugs and alcohol) as a result of coming to Christ. He was reaching out to his old friends like a blind person who had just received his sight and now knew where others could receive deliverance.

2. *Love for the unlovely and the breaking down of socio-economic barriers are attractive qualities of many of these churches.* As we participated in worship at one of these congregations, we could not help noticing the great diversity. The people around us looked like business professionals, truck drivers, indigents, elderly, minorities, students, teenagers, and so forth. Of all the congregations we visited, the charismatic, worship-centered churches had the least socioeconomic uniformity. What bound them together was a strong expectation that God would minister to physical and spiritual needs with dramatic power, and that direct revelation from God (usually through the leader) was to be expected.

3. *Faith to move mountains characterizes many of these ministries.* These churches expect God to act in dramatic ways. Too many of our churches treat God like an antique chair—valuable but not functional. People will sacrifice a lot to keep it (God) but seldom sit on it (trust God to act supernaturally) or encourage others to do so. By contrast, many charismatic congregations dare to trust God to display an authentic power that the world cannot easily explain and often knows nothing about. They seem undaunted by the fact that some prayers seem to go unanswered. Somehow they know that power is available even if we cannot always tap into it. The expectation of spiritual power inspires worship and praise.

4. *Joy and zeal in worship were always present in the charismatic churches that we visited.* In many of these worship-centered congregations it is not uncommon for believers to spend as much as ninety minutes in praise and worship where the only attraction is God—no special entertainment, no provocative sermon, no dramatic ministry—just worship. And this worship does not drag. It is full of joy and wonder; it is not a funeral dirge or a meaningless, outdated ritual. As one charismatic friend put it, "Our brand of Christianity is not any better than anyone else's; we just enjoy it more."

Concerns

The charismatic, worship-centered church, however, raises some concerns. While many congregations manage to avoid the following pitfalls, questions remain as we reflect on the nondenominational charismatic congregations that we have known. It should be noted that the charismatic churches that are the focus of this critique are to be distinguished from classic Pentecostal denominations that more often have recognized the need to address these concerns.

1. How does one handle conflicting messages "from God"? How does one deal with the confusion when too much regard is given to "special revelations," especially when no consensus can be reached, or even worse, when consensus is reached but is contrary to God's true will? We have personally witnessed one church split three times because of leaders with different "words from God." Shepherds among God's people must be able to hear from God and at the same time humbly submit to the whole body of Christ.

Also, how can one avoid the tendency to equate the presence of powerful answers to a leader's prayer with the carte blanche blessing of God on anything that leader believes or practices? One of the confusing characteristics of the rise and fall of charismatic TV evangelists is the continued confidence that their followers seem to have in their leadership in spite of their shameful conduct. Could it be that the real test of God's favor on these men, in the eyes of their followers, is their ability to stir the souls of others with their charisma? Their character and conduct seem to be incidental. As long as "I can feel the Spirit" when he ministers, "I will support him because he still must have 'the anointing.'" This attitude seems too much like the negative side of the Corinthian church that we do not want to emulate.

2. Are healthy, self-critical skills being cultivated? This concern is related to number one above. What checks and balances exist for leaders who fail to be self-critical or accountable to the whole body of Christ? How can people in these churches be encouraged to develop healthy, critical thinking and be kept from blindly following powerful but misguided leaders? After all, if I am convinced that God has spoken directly to me or to my leader, why should I ask questions? Who wants to be in danger of arguing with God? We must find a way in which we can take God very seriously without taking ourselves too seriously. We need to be able to affirm that not only has God's Spirit spoken, but also humbly admit that we may be hard-of-hearing or imperfect prophets.

3. Must spiritual power always be dramatic? Do we neglect the more routine, disciplined process of spiritual growth when we focus only on God's dramatic acts? One of the things we looked for in all of the reaching-up congregations that we visited was a healthy respect for the "process." Do we respect the fact that God often works through the mundane and even the natural avenues to heal and reveal? Does God always have to use spiritual special effects?

Too often we have seen dramatic, short-term responses that were not an accurate indication of the true, long-term effect. In one particular congregation, the people seemed to live from one worship high to another with (1) little real service to others as an act of worship during the week or (2) little personal, character growth over several years.

4. What happens when faith becomes a demanding spirit? Do we tend to place too much emphasis on our faith? Must we insist that the only obstacle between God's promise and my experience is our faith? Is it not true that God's timing and our possible misunderstanding of his word may be factors in why life does not work as expected? Or can a person trust God and yet say, "Thy will be done"? Can true, living faith be sometimes active and other times passive? That is, can I trust God to be with me and support me *through* a hard time as well as deliver me *from* a hard time? Is it not true that although faith can move mountains, God sometimes asks us to bear burdens?

5. Is too little attention given to sound historical and theological truths? The danger of letting the tail of experience wag the dog of sound theology is always present in ministries that emphasize tangible experience. Just because some Christians have neglected the cultivation of a deep and rich experiential faith does not mean that their emphasis on academic theology was the problem. The often quoted statement, "Doctrine divides; the Spirit unites," can be misleading. Except for the mystic individual, all spiritual experience seeks for some kind of reflective critique.

In some charismatically oriented churches, the inconsistency between the strong love expressed for those who share the emphasis of the "in group" and the equally dramatic distrust and disdain for those Christians who do not is conspicuous.

A careful study of history and culture can be humbling for those who assume that they have easy or pat answers to faith and faithfulness. The dramatic spiritual experiences (including speaking in tongues) of non-Christian faiths, and the inconsistencies of some charismatic congregations with historic Christianity should cause us to be careful in our conclusions and responses to spiritual experiences, no matter how dramatic.

6. Is it possible to be too preoccupied with the present blessings of God? Do we make room for a place to wait, forbear, and even suffer in this life? Must all the blessings of God be experienced now? It is striking to see how much of the New Testament's message is centered in hope. History reminds us that devout Christians have often lived lives of faith while enduring great suffering and disappointment. In some charismatic congregations, one gets the impression that a theology of suffering and pain in this life does not exist. It is as though the devil is behind anything that we do not like and God is for everything that we want. The issue is then centered on *our* faith to release what we want from God and banish from our present experience the devil and all the things we do not like. This sounds too much like the spirit of our age, and not at all like the Spirit of Christ.

7. Can a church be too sensate-oriented? A tendency in ministry and spirituality to be too responsive to the five senses is present in each style, but especially in the worship-centered church. This question reflects the most basic concern that we have. As one charismatic leader put it, "We have a theology of practice, not a theology of propositions." He went on to say that what we understand with our mind or say with our mouth is only important insofar as it bears fruit in our hearts (emotions) and our walk (experiences). In other words, if we do not feel it or see it, we are not impressed with it. This form of Christianity is centered in the five senses. It is sensual.

At a time when so many of our congregations are sense-less in their worship, a correction is in order. But a sensual orientation can lead to a very restricted view of worship in which believers only sense they really worship when and if they feel or experience certain things. Any other expression of worship may be viewed as less than authentic. We talked to some people in worship-centered congregations who were critical of worshipers who do not raise their hands or feel deep emotions while praising God. One leader suggested to me that people who do not manifest certain outward characteristics in their worship are not really worshiping. They may be praising God (in the flesh), but they are not "experiencing worship in the Spirit."

The charismatic renewal has reawakened God's people to his living, dynamic presence in space and time. However, with this exciting renewal, a new or perhaps old Corinthian tendency, a demanding spirit of sensual Christianity, may appear. Sensual preoccupation is concerned with the present more than the future, the dramatic more than the usual, the emotional, subjective sense more than the rational, objective sense.

If we could give one word of advice to the charismatic, worship-centered church, it would be: Put your best foot forward, but don't kick your neighbor or lose your balance. In other words, show the rest of the church how to worship and trust God. Do this with your actions and with a humble, servant-oriented spirit, not with a lecture on what you have and the rest of us should have but do not. As you put your best foot forward, be careful not to stumble so as to lead people to false expectations. Seek to be respected for your servants' hearts, not for your spiritual special effects. Do not act as though the rest of us are second-class citizens, guilty of quenching the Spirit, if we do not agree to parts of your theology or share your emphasis. Be a blessing to us, not a curse.

THE REACHING-UP CHURCH

Strengths
- Boldness and confidence in ministry
- Love for the unlovely
- Faith to move mountains
- Joy and zeal in worship

Concerns
- Conflicting, special revelation
- A lack of self-critical skills
- A preoccupation with the dramatic
- A demanding spirit
- A weak, theological foundation
- A preoccupation with the present
- A sensate orientation

Examine Yourself

1. Is your church a worship-centered congregation? How would you know? Are you pleased with this emphasis?
2. If your church is a charismatic, worship-centered church, are you in touch with the strengths and weaknesses of your style?
3. Can you offer to the broader, Christian community your assets in ministry without judging them or insulting their strengths or emphasis, which may be different from yours?
4. How can you help the rest of the church worship without offending those who might not share certain distinctives of your theology?
5. How would you assess the strengths and concerns expressed in this chapter? What would you add or delete?

4.

THE REACHING-DOWN (BIBLE-TEACHING) CHURCH

EXPOSITING THE BIBLE FAITHFULLY

The second style of congregation we will look at is the "feeding station" or Bible-teaching church. My own spiritual growth has been tied to this style of church more than to any other. It was the clear and practical teaching of the Bible that got my attention as a university student. I was a nominal Christian who had generally dismissed the Bible as irrelevant in any practical way to my life. One day I accompanied a friend to a Bible-teaching church and was captivated by what the pastor was saying as he guided the congregation through a verse-by-verse explanation of one of Paul's letters. I had never heard this kind of teaching before, and it drew me back to the church and a serious commitment to Christ. I also can say that my interest has not waned as I have seen my faith and hope in Christ grow through exposure to fresh insights from God's Word. As I have had to face difficulties such as raising a son who has autism and helping others face disappointments and fractured relationships, I have found the Bible-teaching church's emphasis on clear, expositional teaching from Scripture to be very practical and powerful in building a deeper and richer faith.

The reaching-down (Bible-teaching) congregations range in size from the very small (less than one hundred members) to the very large, such as Grace Community Church in Sun Valley, California, with a membership of several thousand. Congregations of this type center their ministry around expository Bible-teaching. Although some Presbyterian, Baptist, and other denominationally affiliated congregations fit into this category, the most typical model is the independent, nondenominational Bible Church. They may go by any one of a number of names—Community Church and Bible Church being the most common. These congregations are not affiliated within an organization, but their style is similar and unmistakable. Teaching or preaching the Word is the central function of this church's ministry.

Berea

The Bereans were noted in the book of Acts (17:10-12) for their noble-mindedness, eager reception of the Word, and diligence in examining the Scriptures to see if what they were hearing from the speaker/teacher was true. Down through the years hundreds of churches have aspired to deserve the same reputation. A love for truth as presented in the Scriptures is what marked the disciples in Berea, and it is a mark worn by many congregations today. As in the book of Acts, where Berea stood in stark contrast to the traditionalism of Thessalonica, so today the Bible-teaching congregations are not afraid to turn from denominational traditions that do not find support in Scripture. They tend to be nondenominational. If a part of a denomination, they are often viewed as a bit unconventional.

Characteristics

As in many other styles, the *pulpit ministry* is central in the reaching-down church. Though the ministry of the Word is central to most Protestant congregations, in this style of ministry the church is typically more teaching than preaching oriented. Sometimes the Sunday service looks and feels like a Sunday school class, with people taking notes or even receiving outlines with the bulletin. In some worship services, time is allowed after the sermon (lecture) for a period of questions and answers from the floor.

The teachers in this type of church are usually gifted communicators with impressive knowledge of biblical data and a very logical, outlined approach in their delivery. These churches often shy away from emotional appeals or political calls for action, but instead concentrate their attention on what one pastor described as "getting Bible doctrine in the frontal lobe" of the brain. In this respect, the Bible-teaching church is different from the fire-and-brimstone, fundamentalist church that also places a premium on the pulpit ministry. The fire-and-brimstone congregations are more appropriately placed with the reaching-back churches to be examined in chapter 7.

The importance of Bible teaching will be apparent throughout these churches' programs. Virtually every meeting will include some sort of Bible reading and exposition. The annual business meeting will probably start with the reading of Scripture and a brief point of exposition from the pastor. A prayer meeting will include some form of exposition. The praise and worship on Sunday morning will focus attention on the message, or more often settle people in for the teaching of the Word. The Sunday school program will be geared to teaching children and adults directly from the Bible.

When asked to identify the marks of a good church, members of the Bible-teaching congregation will often respond with "good exposition of the Bible" as the number one criteria. On one occasion, we heard a pastor ask one of his friends a question about a neighboring church. "Does the church preach expositionally, verse-by-verse?" That was all he wanted to know as he sized up the value of another congregation's ministry. If it exposited the Word, it was on track, and if it did not, it was not seen as offering much of any value.

The Bible-teaching churches take a literal approach to the Bible with a strong emphasis on the inerrancy of Scripture. Sometimes these churches will have very detailed doctrinal statements with even more complex, unwritten traditions in their teaching. People in the congregation, pastors/leaders and members alike, are expected to know the Bible even if they do not know the person sitting next to them or the creeds of the ancient church.

These congregations stand firm against modernity's inflated confidence in scientific materialism and also against postmodernity's spurning of the whole notion of absolute, public truth. As they surround themselves with like-minded believers who ask few questions and take lots of notes, the pastors and parishioners in the teaching-centered church are often not even aware of the winds of modernity and postmodernity.

A literal approach to the Bible is mixed with deep commitment to following in detail its prescriptions. One congregation refused to recognize men who were not married as leaders in "obedience" to Titus 1:6, which mentions "the husband of one wife." When points of policy are made or pastoral decisions are communicated, the church leader is expected to come with a reference to a Bible verse attached for credibility.

Another characteristic is a *deep suspicion of emotionally driven spirituality* because of its subjectivity. In addition, members of these churches have a tendency to be suspicious of ideas that are derived from the secular, scientific community—especially when they do not illustrate popular, biblical teaching. Pop psychology is a particularly suspect field of knowledge.

Many of these congregations have answers from the Bible to virtually any question one might ask concerning life. As a matter of fact, the teachers in these churches are often expected to have answers to all questions. Few mysteries appear to be left once a person is thoroughly taught the Word.

These congregations exalt the role of the teacher above all other ministries in the church, and those who come to these churches often have little interest in ministries that do not in some way enhance their understanding of the Bible.

Examples

In Escondido, California, the late Richard Strauss, pastor of the large Emmanuel Faith Community Church, was a powerful example of this type of ministry. This congregation is more conservative and traditional in style than many large, growing congregations, but it is no less effective. It was clear from everyone we met at this congregation that expository Bible teaching was at the core of its ministry. Richard Strauss, a gifted teacher—humble, clear, down-to-earth, and in touch with people's hurts—was revered by all.

You could see the effect of his ministry in people's enthusiasm not only for his teaching, but also for his ministry in a wide range of other areas—youth, parents, singles. This congregation had dozens of programs targeting almost any need anyone might have, from managing personal finances and reaching out to the poor in the community to recovering from substance abuse. But the emphasis in this congregation was obvious—expository Bible teaching.

· We met a number of individuals who became Christians in fast-growing, outreach-oriented churches but who wound up in the feeding-station, Bible-teaching churches, where they felt they could mature further. They tended to be initially attracted to the more energetic and entertaining approach of market-driven churches (which we will look at later), but after several months they found the Bible-teaching churches to be satisfying their hunger for God's Word and bringing them to a deeper level in their spiritual lives.

Strengths

1. These congregations teach the Scriptures with confidence at a time and in a cultural context in which such a ministry has lost its favor in some mainline churches. These congregations believe not only that the truth of the biblical record is absolute, but also that it can be communicated through careful exposition. The popularity of these churches can be attributed to (a) the great hunger among God's people for a practical understanding of the Bible and (b) an expositional approach to the Bible. The expository approach of teaching adopted by many of the reaching-down churches forces the preacher or teacher to deal with difficult passages. People respect this honest and courageous approach in that it helps laypeople in their understanding as they read the Bible. In some ways it might be said that a careful exposition of a whole book of the Bible is at the heart of what the Bible-teaching church has to offer.

2. Another strength of these congregations is their serious defense of the authority and practical value of the Scriptures. The teaching pastor believes and teaches biblical truths as though they were a life-or-death issue. He builds a person's faith in God by showing how the Scripture is relevant to everyday life. He links life and people directly with a biblical text with specific clear instructions as to how to respond or what to believe. As one young woman shared, "I come to this church because, for the first time, I have the Bible explained to me in such a way that I can apply it directly to my job and family relationships."

The Bible-teaching congregation is often suspicious of problem-solving techniques that originate from the secular arena. For example, they will often discard widely accepted and popular theories from modern psychology, biology, business, and so forth. They believe that the Bible is enough and that it contains all the really important information that they need to deal with life's challenges.

3. These congregations build into people's lives a foundation of understanding that proves invaluable for permanent growth and endurance through the trials of life. Many of the people we have met from these congregations demonstrated an ability to face the storms of life with a confidence and peace that was impressive. These people were not ignorant of the complexities of life, but yet they had a well-defined hope that was centered neither in the circumstances of this life nor in an emotional experience, but in the biblical promise of God's kingdom to come. They were not easily swayed by every crisis or powerful experience or wind of doctrine.

Concerns

1. Can Bible teaching be just a head trip? Is love for the written Word synonymous with love for the Living Word? Is intellectual understanding of the truth rewarded or admired by members of these churches even when it is not applied or integrated deeply into life? As many of us know, a love for the Bible may not translate into a love for God or God's people. The church needs to avoid emphasizing a great love for Bible content at the expense of knowing and following Christ. Sometimes we have sensed that people equate the two. Truth that is not experienced is no better than error, and may be equally as dangerous.

2. Is teaching the only thing that counts? As we visited with one of the staff of a well-known Bible church, we were told that "the pastor recognizes the diversity of gifts in the church but leaves the impression that the only gift that really counts is the gift of teaching." But what about worship? Does worship have its own significance, or is it a sort of pre-game warm-up for the teaching? Sometimes in Bible-teaching churches, our impression was that praise and worship were optional or even fluff, while the only real action was the sermon. Our sense is that the exposition should be the catalyst to worship, not the other way around. One thing can be said from our real life experiences: Knowing the doctrines of the Bible and being committed to doing all we can to live by them, though noble and important, is not enough to bring us to maturity in Christ. A subjective, passionate encounter with the Living Christ through his Spirit must also be present.

3. Do we put God in a box? How do we keep from reducing truth to propositional categories and tight linear logic, leaving little room for mystery, awe, or process? Is all truth confined to the Bible? Are we not to learn also from science, history, and personal experience? Can Bible expositors really have as much dogmatic certainty as they seem to portray? Are we putting God in a box where God can never surprise us with something that we do not understand or expect? One pastor, when asked about his devotional life, said, "I just reviewed my notes on doctrine." The impression he left was that he had discovered all there was to know and that now it was just a matter of reviewing his notes. If this is what a personal relationship with the living Lord of the universe is all about, we need help.

4. Does Bible knowledge puff up spiritual couch potatoes or produce humble, active servants? When the focus is on learning about the things of God, is it not easy to equate one's status in the community with one's knowledge of doctrine? It is not uncommon for Bible-teaching churches to be more impressed with new insights into objective, scriptural truth than insights into the subjective dynamic of a relationship with God and others. How many people would come to a meeting in a Bible-teaching church if the only agenda was praise and worship—no teaching? We need to hunger for faith, hope, and love more than biblical outlines, Greek terms, and memorized verses. Is not the real test of biblical education spiritual liberation to selfless service and vibrant worship of God? Until that is achieved, all the teaching and knowledge that we can absorb may be more impressive to us than to God.

5. *Do we ignore the ambiguities of different interpretations?* In Bible-teaching churches it is often assumed that if one has a high view of Scripture, that is, if he or she believes that the Bible is inspired and inerrant, few questions as to its meaning and application will follow. In some reaching-down congregations, a lot of time can be spent defending the inerrancy of the Bible while the critical issues of differences in interpretation and application are ignored. It must be realized that many people who believe that the Bible is inerrant from the first chapters of Genesis to the last chapters of Revelation cannot agree on what Genesis and Revelation mean. What so often happens in a congregation of this type is the enthronement of the teaching pastor as a local mini-pope. His interpretation, which even if arbitrary and inaccurate, is seldom in doubt and often unquestioned by his followers. Many, if not most Bible-teaching churches, follow a dogmatic, dispensational approach to interpretation. How can they be so certain that such a literal approach is really sound?

6. *Are the hard questions of modern and postmodern culture being ignored?* How does the average Bible-teaching church help someone who is influenced by postmodern thinking, in which there is no absolute truth, just relative and private opinion? Is it effective to just proclaim, "The Bible says . . ."? Sometimes we have gotten the impression that leaders in the teaching-centered congregations are living in a different cultural age altogether. Some of them seem to be unaware of all but the most superficial aspects of what is taking place in the secular culture. But then again, the individuals that they attract and address often

share their premodern perspective. We need both solid biblical teaching and also help in applying it to modern life.

If we can leave one word of advice with the Bible-teaching church, it would be, put your best foot forward without kicking your neighbor or losing your balance. Be as impassioned about knowing God as you are about knowing about God. Do not judge the rest of the church by how much they know, but rather by how much they practice what they know. Teach us the Word, but remind us that the Christian walk consists of more than giving and receiving good teaching. And when you teach, address the real needs of modern life with faithful insight and sensitive concern. In short, show us how the biblical material is relevant for our lives today.

THE REACHING-DOWN CHURCH

Strengths
- Confidence in Scripture
- Defense of biblical authority
- Building a solid foundation

Concerns
- Is this just a head trip?
- Is teaching the only gift that counts?
- Is God put in a doctrinal box?
- Is the goal life-style or just understanding?
- Is there a tendency to ignore diverse interpretations?
- Is the modern culture ignored?

Examine Yourself

1. To what extent does this style of ministry describe your church? Where does your congregation differ from the above description?
2. If you are in a Bible-teaching church, have you been able to avoid some of the concerns expressed above? Where do you feel your church is most vulnerable? How can needed changes be made?
3. What are the greatest personal benefits for you in the Bible-teaching church? How can you preserve the strengths while avoiding the liabilities of this type of ministry?
4. How can the strengths of the Bible-teaching style of ministry be picked up by congregations that may not now have this emphasis? To what extent is a "gifted teacher" key to this model?
5. Can a congregation have an effective "reaching-down," Bible-teaching emphasis without being locked into a particular view of the inerrancy of the Bible? Does a certain kind of theology go hand in hand with the Bible-teaching church?
6. How would you assess the strengths and concerns expressed in this chapter? What would you add or delete?

5.

The Reaching-In (Relational) Church

Caring for People with Grace and Love

As never before, we are a generation in pursuit of personal peace and happiness. Most American churchgoers want to be happy, healthy, and holy—in that order. If we expect people to pursue holiness, it better be made clear that happiness and emotional/physical health are a guaranteed result. Relationships are a vital part of any church. Relationships are key to personal well-being.

The third category of congregation that we will look at can be called the *koinonia* or relational church. If the worship-centered church is a choir and the teaching-centered church is a class-room, the relational church is a community or family. The organized Christian community or formal commune is the more dramatic expression of the reaching-in church. The more common and popular version is the conventional congregation with a style that is very relational and gracious. We saw more of the conventional congregation than the commune on our visits.

Jerusalem

The first description of the church in Jerusalem after Pentecost represented, at least in the brief description of Acts 2, a dramatic example of the reaching-in style of church. Nowhere else do we see such a powerful example of communal spirit where "they would sell their possessions and goods and distribute the proceeds to all, as any had need" (Acts 2:45 and 4:34).

Successful contemporary models of Christian communal living like Reba Place Fellowship in Evanston, Illinois, are unusual. They are challenged by a secular society, which, on the one hand, is not hostile enough to force people into such a life-style and, on the other, is not helpful enough to make this "radical sacrifice" plausible for most Christians. Relational churches are not to be confused with Christian communes except to say that they share and aspire to a strong sense of community.

Characteristics

The more conventional reaching-in congregations that we saw fell into two types, *affirming relationship* churches and the *mercy ministry* churches. They share the common characteristic of putting people above programs, property, and productivity. If Christ's church can be compared to a family business, then the reaching-in church is heavier on the family side than the business side. These congregations are far less concerned about looking efficient and reaching goals than they are about meeting and ministering to people in the context of a family atmosphere. In church-growth terms they are more a modality than a sodality. That is to say, they tend to be more like a family of nurturing relationships than an army or business trying to reach a tangible objective. Their objective is to create a loving, sensitive, and affirming environment where Christian, interpersonal relationships are the most important issue.

How many of us have wondered: Is it safe for me to be honest with the people in my church? What will happen when they see that I have failed and am motivated by fear of rejection? Are they like me or do they have it all together and just tolerate people like me? These questions and others are asked by most of us. The reaching-in church offers a safe place for those who are stressed by guilt, fear, abuse, and isolation. *Grace, in word and deed, is an important part of the reaching-in congregation.*

Many of the people who flock to the reaching-in congregations are coming from other congregations where they have been stressed by a performance model, a model that made them feel as though they had to take aspirin to kill the pain and put on makeup to hide the tears before they could be welcomed as full members of the church. As one person put it, "If I were honest about my struggles, my church would apply a quick fix and then when it didn't work, would emotionally shut me out as a leper."

The relational church not only puts a high priority on relationships and emphasizes grace, but also *accepts people in process*. It is not uncommon to find, as we did, in these congregations people with long-standing, emotional handicaps. However, these handicaps did not prevent them from being loved and included, in spite of their inability to make dramatic contributions to the program.

The relational congregations were also sensitive to the need for *wholeness* as well as *holiness*. They recognized that until a person sensed their wholeness in Christ and were set free from selfishly driven defenses and strategies of social manipulation, they could not give themselves to selfless service and love of others. It is not enough for many of us to hear about God's love; we need help in sensing it at a deep enough level to set us free from defensive self-centeredness. These congregations were willing to incarnate that love, to demonstrate God's love as well as proclaim it.

Examples

Menlo Park Presbyterian Church in an affluent community south of San Francisco might best fit the category of a relational congregation. The warm, personal style of the senior pastor and worship services have drawn many people to drink the soothing water of God's love and grace. It calls itself a love-driven church where every person is challenged to experience and express God's love.

Some congregations preach about grace and then, in church relationships and programs, send the message that the fine print is a very conditional basis of social acceptance. That atmosphere was not present at Menlo Park. This was a safe place to fail, hurt, struggle, and be honest without fear of rejection.

This congregation of more than three thousand has 60 percent of its people in small support groups that meet during the week. Every meeting at Menlo Park intentionally connects people to God and other people. Ministries are geared to "station" and "crisis-in-life" issues. One of the staff explained, "We try to speak to people in their most teachable states: (1) where they struggle to succeed in the world and (2) when their world crashes in on them."

The second type of reaching-in church focuses on mercy ministries. Trinity Church in Seattle stands in contrast to Menlo Park with respect to its constituents. Trinity has drawn together a group of families into a close community based on their commitment to minister personally and individually to the down-and-outers of their area. This church has been described as "a human salvage yard," not very pretty in the world's eyes, but certainly attractive to anyone in touch with the Spirit of Christ. This place is for those who have been left behind in the rat race of society—the addicts, the homeless, the emotionally abused, and the "orphans and widows" of our modern world.

The stress in this congregation is produced not by performing well before thousands of attenders on Sunday morning, but rather by living with six foster children in a double-wide mobile home, as does one of the pastors.

As we met with key families at Trinity we were received graciously, and we sensed an immediate rapport. When we asked about the Christian education of their children, they replied that they did not emphasize written curriculum; instead they wanted their children to watch the parents reach out to and take in needy people. They felt that if their children grew up seeing God's heart in their homes, they would be drawn to God and eventually seek to know everything they needed to know about Jesus. They, of course, were not suggesting that theological content was unimportant, just that it was best learned in the laboratory of real life.

Strengths

1. These churches foster high-touch environments. Christians in the reaching-in congregations expect to teach through their acceptance and their care of people. These churches provide many opportunities to interact with others about life and faith. They seek to network souls.

2. Grace is not only talked about, it is practiced. They know that many "churched" individuals have heard about God's grace but have never seen it or sensed it at a very deep level. In these churches a hunger for an understanding of an incarnational witness to grace constitutes a vital element in personal spiritual growth and healing. Relational congregations remove the front-loading of the gospel (requiring that people change their lives before they can be considered a believer). They do not mix law and grace. They give people room to be honest, to grow up, and to integrate their faith into their lives over time.

3. The relational church understands the pain of living in a chaotic, fallen world and provides a safe respite from the storms of this life. These congregations may have less aggressive evangelistic growth, but they have a deeper sense of internal community. They attract Christians who have been burned out and wounded, sometimes from overinvolvement in more performance-oriented ministries. As one person put it, "I have become a mile wide and an inch deep. Now I need a place that will listen to my hurts and not just keep challenging me to help the pastor reach his goals."

4. *Small support groups are often a vital part of the pastoral strategy of the relational church.* These groups are not designed to be evangelistic so much as therapeutic healing experiences for those in them. However, as some congregations are discovering, such groups can be a most effective tool in introducing people to Christ.

5. *Honesty is possible in the reaching-in church at levels that may be more threatening in other styles of ministry.* It is believed that until we are honest with ourselves, God, and others, we will not really grow. This honesty, however, is often very painful and difficult to achieve. It requires long-term patience and a willingness to pick up pieces when carefully constructed images of oneself are shattered. In many relational churches it is not uncommon to find people (even the staff) talking openly about their therapy or counseling.

6. *Another plus of the relational church is its emphasis on inner being rather than outward doing.* An inside-out spirituality is cultivated in these congregations. These churches are concerned about inner motives and attitudes—not just how a person looks on the outside. This is not to say that everyone stands around looking at their navel or that things are done in a haphazard way. Often a high level of commitment to service is motivated by love and acceptance rather than fear and guilt. Here individuals are free to fail in ministry without harsh social consequences. As a result, these congregations attract many people who have failed and are wounded and broken—the kind of people that were also attracted to Jesus in the New Testament.

Concerns

Our lingering questions of the reaching-in church center around keeping the delicate balance between unconditional acceptance and the inherent exclusiveness of God's kingdom.

1. Can an inward-reaching congregation be relational in style without sacrificing truth at the altar of love? Can these churches fall into the trap of being more committed to emotional wholeness than spiritual holiness? Or can they, like the secular world, see spiritual holiness as, in some cases, contrary to emotional wholeness? For instance, we never did get a clear answer in some of these congregations when we asked, "When did you last exercise church discipline, and how did you do it?" We were left with the impression that any kind of correction would be perceived as rejection, and the threat of exclusion was incompatible with the overarching goal of love. In some of these congregations, insensitivity or intolerance seemed to meet with more official disapproval than immorality or apostasy. In what ways do these churches present the cost of discipleship (dying to self)? In what ways are such congregations distinct from the secular culture, which has abandoned absolute truth as psychologically abusive to the autonomous self?

2. Is psychological wholeness the bottom line of the Christian life? Is Christ simply an instrument to emotional health? Has Christianity lost its intrinsic worth and taken on the purely instrumental value of helping us cope? As one friend put it concerning a popular self-help sales strategy, "Amway can change your life, but that doesn't mean it is of God." Are we so preoccupied with meeting emotional needs, alleviating temporal anxiety, and medicating social pain that we lose sight of the fact that God is calling us to self-sacrifice and not necessarily happiness? Is God's primary purpose in our lives the removal of all pain?

3. We also wondered whether these congregations did not exclude certain types of people. In the mercy ministry congregations, for instance, we wondered if a person could fit in without either (1) an identifiable dysfunction ("What support group do I join?") or (2) the skill, commitment, and passion necessary to work with the dysfunctional. In some congregations we sensed very little tolerance of anyone who was less tolerant. In some compassion-centered congregations we wondered if prophetic ministries like that of Jeremiah and Isaiah would be tolerated, let alone received or encouraged.

4. Do we neglect discipleship when we are preoccupied with the immediate felt need? In a crisis we must administer first aid, but to build long-term health we must also address life-style, world view, and theological foundation issues. How do we get these issues into the church's program when the people who show up are emotionally starving? Our experience has been that many hurting people demand some immediate quick fix, or they lose interest and move on. We live in a pragmatic, impatient, conversion-prone age, in which people check in and out of belief systems as often as they change jobs, mates, addresses, and churches. In such a context it is too tempting for the church to spend all its energy addressing divorce, drug abuse, or a dysfunctional background on a short-term basis. We must find a way to address the deep, long-term, spiritual needs of people while also providing practical advice for the short-term pains of life. We are finding that most of the struggles that people bring to the church are complex and may require major life overhauls. However, in the face of any crisis, individuals need enough hope to stay around long enough to have their inner lives renewed.

5. In an age when autonomy is so pervasive and popular, how can people be held accountable? It is easier to hide in our present culture than ever before, and it is often seen as intrusive or even unethical to get involved too closely in disciplining another person. The relational church is sometimes supersensitive to being legalistic, but at what expense? Many of us need more controls and boundaries without the spirit of legalism or fear of rejection. Can the relational church meet that need?

If we could leave one word of advice with the relational church, it would be—continue to convict and teach the rest of the church of its need to minister to struggling saints. Put your best foot forward. Show the church how powerful the doctrine of grace can be when it is demonstrated. In an age when so many Christians are needy, it is vital that we slow down, listen, share, and find the grace to help. However, while you are demonstrating grace in action, be careful to avoid having your strength discredited by failing to hold fast to basic distinctives of Christian doctrine and deportment. Do not lose your balance or kick your neighbor. Do not lose your compassion for the less compassionate. Some other congregations seem too ready to default to impersonal law out of fear of grace without standards. Show them that radical grace and love need not threaten our high calling to holiness.

THE REACHING-IN CHURCH

Strengths

• High touch	• Small groups
• Grace	• Honesty
• Safe respite	• Slower pace

Concerns

- Love over truth
- Wholeness over holiness
- Exclusivity
- Discipleship
- Accountability

Examine Yourself

1. To what extent is your church a relational church? Why or why not?
2. If your congregation has several of the qualities of a relational church, what has contributed to their development? What might threaten them?
3. Is your church vulnerable to any of the concerns expressed about reaching-in churches? Which ones? How can these potential pitfalls be avoided?
4. Do you agree with the assessment of this chapter? What would you add to the section on strengths? What would you add to the section on concerns?

6.

THE REACHING-OUT (MARKET-DRIVEN) CHURCH

COMMUNICATING THE MESSAGE OF THE GOSPEL

Lee Iacocca, former CEO of an auto company, reportedly said, "The ideal car is designed in Europe, manufactured in Japan, and marketed in the U.S.A." If Americans know how to do one thing better than anyone else, it is selling. We know how to market, package, advertise, and close the sale. Can this marketing genius in our culture be as useful to the church as it is to business? Should the church ignore it, ban it, or use it? The impact of marketing expertise and church growth philosophy on the evangelistic call to God's people is well documented and needs no introduction.

Athens

The ministry of Paul in Athens is remembered for its intellectual and philosophical emphasis (Acts 17:16-31). He breaks from his usual pattern of arguing from Hebrew Scriptures or the historical fact of the cross and resurrection to speak in terms of the Athenian's world of ideas and gods. What the careful observer of Paul's method notes is his use of contextualization, the application of his understanding of the Athenian culture to the shaping of his ministry methods. The approach Paul used in Athens might not have been appropriate in Jerusalem or Thessalonica. It is this sensitivity to the audience and flexibility in method that illustrate the market-driven style of ministry. It is not surprising to note that just as Paul's methods in Athens have been criticized by students of the Scriptures down through the ages, so are modern examples of contextualization falling under critical scrutiny today. How far can and should the church go to win the world's ear?

Characteristics

First, the market-driven church most often sees evangelism as its primary calling. Other functions of the church constitute preparation for or follow-up to reaching non-Christians with the message of the gospel.

Second, these congregations are concerned about reaching a targeted, non-Christian, culturally homogeneous audience with the gospel in a user-friendly way. They are willing to study their targeted audience's language, style of life, felt needs, and responses to data and then use that knowledge in packaging the gospel message for them. Market-driven churches are usually conservative and evangelical in their theology, yet free in the use of sociological, psychological, and demographic data for shaping their ministries.

Third, these churches are very free and creative in finding practical and effective ways to reach their targeted audience. As one pastor put it, "If it works we are open to trying it." For example, it is not uncommon to see the Sunday morning service (or in some cases Saturday night service) turned into what is called a "seeker-service," designed for the non-Christian who is not comfortable in a traditional worship setting. This service may be void of religious jargon, symbols, and liturgies, all of which are replaced with drama presentations, contemporary music, and short, practical biblical messages.

Fourth, these congregations are geared up for fast, long-term growth. They expect to grow. They take risks to grow. They work hard to grow. And they usually grow. They can spring up in a bedroom, suburban community and grow from a dozen families to several hundred or even thousands of members in a matter of a few years.

Examples

Willow Creek Community Church, pastored by Bill Hybels, is perhaps the most prominent example of this style of ministry. Willow Creek targets young, unchurched, urban professionals in an affluent suburb of Chicago. So much publicity has surrounded this one congregation that it needs no further introduction. Starting with a handful of believers in 1975, it now draws over fourteen thousand people to its weekend services.

The service we attended on our sabbatical modeled its strategy. Contemporary music was performed, a drama was presented, and an interview was conducted with three church members who were enduring physical suffering at the time. Bill asked them, "What is it like?" and "How has Christ made a difference?" They responded candidly and with hope, yet without simplistic resolution of their difficulties. Bill followed with a short, biblical message on finding God in the midst of our suffering.

Of all the services we visited during the sabbatical, this service most impressed our two teenage children.

As we talked to individuals behind the scenes at Willow Creek, we were struck by their careful attention to detail and their well-defined focus on reaching their target audience (thirty-five-year-old, unchurched males). We received permission to attend a rehearsal for the Saturday evening service, a privilege comparable to attending one of Coach Dean Smith's basketball practices in Chapel Hill! The rehearsal schedule was printed out to the minute and followed to the letter.

As we walked through the spacious halls of the facilities at Willow Creek with one of the staff, we noticed a hand smudge near a cleaning closet. We were told that it would be scrubbed off or painted over before the next service. We were reminded that "Young executives go to work every day in a world that does not tolerate smudges. When they come here, we want them to say, 'Hey, these people care as much about their ministry as my company does about my business.' "

Willow Creek is a phenomenon that deserves its high profile among the churches that seek to speak the language of a modern, baby-boomer culture.

Strengths

1. These congregations focus on people and culture. In some other congregations, traditional programs, doctrines, and methods so occupy the attention of the church that present realities about people and their culture are ignored. On the other hand, the market-driven congregations that we saw tied spiritual truths to life's realities. These congregations give lots of attention to practical, felt needs such as coping with marketplace stress, raising children in single-parent households, and managing credit. Sermons, classes, seminars, and ministry teams are used to address these and other felt needs.

2. These congregations are unusually sensitive to the stewardship of resources. The market-driven congregations remind us of our freedom to be creative, resourceful, and practical with talents, programs, and so forth. Efficiency is most desirable, and the best management skills available are brought to bear in solving the challenges of a growing congregation. While it is too often the case that a congregation is unwilling to make creative decisions, the market-driven church leads the way in this area. If something does not contribute to reaching a particular goal and is not fundamental to the faith, it is changed or discarded in favor of something that works. All of this is done without regret.

3. These congregations are successful in outreach. They ask the question: What will work to reach people and bring about a desired response? Attention is given by church leaders to the subculture targeted to be reached. (Not all subcultures are suburban and yuppie. Some of these leaders target the homeless or the illiterate in rural areas.) The leaders put themselves in the place of individuals outside the church and ask questions such as the following: What is it like to walk in their shoes? What are their concerns? What language do they respond to most often? What are their patterns of behavior? How can we get and hold their attention?

4. These congregations have returned evangelistic outreach from parachurch ministries to the church-base. The market-driven church has recaptured confidence in and vision for the local congregation. Most of the people involved in these churches are wildly enthusiastic about their church and have no trouble advertising it with enthusiasm and sincerity. They have a renewed vision of what God can do through the church.

5. These congregations have integrated faith into the marketplace. The market-driven church has insisted that faith be practical and relevant to the people they want to reach. These churches want to address real-life issues and felt needs in practical ways with tangible results. Faith and doctrine are to be applied to every area of life, not hoarded in a file or reserved for church appearances and congregational business meetings.

6. These congregations have demanded tangible results. This focus is perhaps the most powerful testimony to the strength of the market-driven congregation. These churches reach people (lots of people) who otherwise would not be reached. They know how to get a response from their targeted audiences. They are not afraid to go for and demand tangible fruit.

7. *These churches are not afraid to be self-critical about their effectiveness and about the orthodoxy of their message.* These congregations are forever analyzing and evaluating the effectiveness of what they do. One of the unjustified criticisms of market-driven ministries is that they do not really serve up a solid Christian message. We did not find this critique to be valid as we visited several such congregations. The messages and emphases that we encountered were not only creatively presented, but also orthodox, not watered down, and without apology.

8. *The market-driven congregations place a high priority on quality of service.* They seem almost obsessed with excellence as they compete head-to-head with the best the world has to offer in the areas of communication, child care, creature comforts, and information. The market-driven congregation makes an impression that draws the admiration and respect of even the most discriminating man and woman who are looking for professional quality at every level of service.

Concerns

Although we share much of the excitement about the market-driven approach, we do see some points where those who cultivate this style are vulnerable and must be careful. We want to say at the outset that many of the congregations we visited recognized the fine line between faithful fruitfulness and faithless fireworks and were sensitive to most of the issues raised below.

1. *Is the market allowed to dictate too much of the church's agenda?* Church marketing is driven more by results than theology or personal experience, and therein lies its weakness and strength. While the market-driven congregation is almost always

willing to critically assess its effectiveness, is it as willing to critically review the credibility of its basic market-driven philosophy? It is one thing to point out that Jesus and the apostles were concerned about marketing issues and quite another to uncritically jump to Madison Avenue as though everything the marketing experts of the world tell us is gospel if it works. While tangible results are important, we must not forget that Jesus was far more concerned about the process and the motives than just getting results. His own ministry by today's marketing standards would be viewed as a disaster.

2. *Is the church aware of how easy it is to manipulate and be manipulated in the marketplace?* When the church engages in marketing, our sense is not that it has become too sophisticated, but that it has not become sophisticated enough to sense the difference between the wind of the Spirit and the spiritually toxic gases of modern advertising. The lemming-like attachment of some church leaders to the latest insights into marketing and managerial expertise suggests that the church might be unaware of the dangers of tapping into modernity's latest tools of manipulation. How many cultural goldfish are we willing to swallow to draw a crowd? How much of that game can the church play without losing its integrity? How much of that game must it play to gain and keep an audience?

3. *Is the process of making true disciples unnecessarily handicapped when people have been evangelized through an "I'll-give-you-what-you-want" ministry?* It is one thing to draw a crowd. It is something else to make true disciples of One who bore a cross and asked his followers to deny themselves. It is not hard to win people if we give them what they want, but how can we then bring them to follow Christ, who leads them where only desperate people are willing to go? Our sense is that a totally market-driven approach may be more successful in evangelism than in disciple making. If we win people with the loss leader of, let's say, secular excellence, can we then renew their minds to

kingdom excellence, which in some ways is at odds with secular values? The typical "baby boomer" says, "I'll pick what meets my needs and drop it when it no longer delivers." But Jesus says, "Take up your cross and follow me." The child of modern culture says, "I want choices." Jesus says, "I am the way, the truth, and the life." The apostles remind us in 1 Corinthians 1:17-31 and James 2:1-9 that the true gospel is going to be a hard sell to those who are deeply committed to the world's values and not fed up with them.

4. Is the church left with a sense of inflated responsibility? When we take too much responsibility, the result can lead to pride if the church succeeds, guilt or despair if it fails, and relative disregard for God's role either way.

Control is a big issue in marketing. The church can adopt a marketing approach that is sensitive to the biblical boundaries of our responsibility, but it is all too tempting to try to play God by feeling responsible for too much. What does God expect the church to control? Are we taking too much responsibility for the response of others? Have we forgotten the parable of the soils (Mark 4:1-20) where disciples are taught to expect negative responses? If there is no sale, secular marketing philosophy never blames the buyer, always the marketer.

5. Does the market-driven philosophy court some questionable priorities? Is evangelism, or reaching the "seeker," the central calling of the church? Is it the means to a greater end (a worshiping community) or is it the end to which all else is a means? The New Testament epistles suggest that outreach is the means to the end, which is best understood as the dynamic church that is focused more on growth and maturity than spiritual birth.

When we "become all things to all people that we might reach them," we understandably adopt some of the tastes, styles, and values of our target audience. For example, *excellence* (defined as productivity and reaching measurable objectives with class), *efficiency* (defined as creatively maximizing resources and gifts), and *quality* (defined as delighting or satisfying aesthetic tastes) are hallmarks of the value structure of a boomer subculture. In showcasing these values, the market-driven church may win the attention and respect of unchurched prospects, but does it transform people from their secular world view to a kingdom perspective, in which the priorities are radically different? In giving people what they want, are we satisfying or stimulating their appetite for the world's answers to life's pain?

God's ways are often contrary to the wisdom of humankind, especially in terms of efficiency and values. For example, Jesus' ministry and the ministry of Paul seem to be very inefficient by today's standards. Do congregations that are committed to cultural excellence recognize the seductive power of idolizing excellence? Do they know that cultural excellence can actually present an obstacle to many people? For example, I recall an annual Christmas talent show at our congregation where the first act was a husband and wife duet on harmonica and guitar. Halfway through the second verse of the song, Christi forgot the words and kept playing her guitar as she sang, "I forgot the words." Her husband calmly turned to the congregation and said, "I haven't forgotten my part" and kept playing the harmonica. The atmosphere was relaxed; they felt safe to mess up because they were with their spiritual family. That relaxed attitude reflected the spirit of Christ's community. Such an atmosphere can be attractive in a stressed-out and graceless world where it is seldom safe to fail. In this case, it made a very positive impression on a visitor who was attending our church for the first time.

Market-Sensitive or Market-Controlled?

If we would leave one word of advice with the market-driven church, it would be—seek to be market-sensitive, but not market-controlled. Put your best foot forward, but do not lose your balance or kick your neighbor. The proper relationship of the church of Christ to its culture is at the heart of the issue. Should the church dance with culture or put out a contract on it? If it does dance with culture, should it let culture lead or should it insist on taking the lead? Our sense is that the church should dance with culture, but never give over the lead.

THE REACHING-OUT CHURCH

Strengths

- Sensitivity to culture
- Stewardship of resources
- Effective outreach to the lost
- Church-based ministry
- Integration of faith
- Tangible results
- Creative approach to ministry
- Quality services

Concerns

- The lordship of marketing
- Manipulation
- Evangelism without discipleship
- Too much human responsibility
- Adoption of questionable priorities

Examine Yourself

1. Is your church a market-driven church? In what way? What are the signs of marketing that you see?

2. Do you agree or disagree with the strengths and concerns expressed in this chapter? What would you add or delete?
3. What do you feel is the greatest asset and greatest liability to a market-driven approach in your setting?
4. To what extent can the church learn and borrow from the business world without losing its soul?

7

THE REACHING-BACK (TRADITIONAL) CHURCH

PRESERVING AND APPRECIATING OUR HERITAGE

The vast majority of the Christian congregations in America fall within the traditional (reaching-back) category or style. While being less influential, they will probably continue to make up a majority of the congregations of the twenty-first century. It is easy for more progressive congregations to be less than charitable in their assessment of the traditional church, but in doing so they overlook much of the rich value of the reaching-back congregation.

Galatia

The Galatian churches of the first century had some of the same characteristics of the modern, reaching-back church. The churches in Galatia were influenced strongly by tradition and the work of God in history. In the case of the Galatian churches, these influences presented some significant problems, some of which characterize many reaching-back congregations in our day as well. A reluctance to break with the traditions and a way of thinking that was a part of a former era marked these churches for harsh rebuke by the apostle Paul. While it is possible for the reaching-back church to be healthy, vibrant, and progressive, it is too often not the case.

To understand this tendency to conserve Jewish culture through the Old Covenant together with the New Covenant in Christ, one must look at the Pharisees of Jesus' day. The Pharisees deserved the respect that they had among the Jews because of their courage to stand against creeping secularism among God's people. However, in their attempt to preserve the true faith, they also fought to preserve the culture that had grown up around it. They failed to see that the wine and the wineskin were two distinct entities. This tendency to equate the wine and the wineskin is a human impulse that continued into much of the early church. It is a challenge for the reaching-back church of today as well.

Characteristics

If you were to ask someone in a reaching-back congregation to describe the characteristics of a good church, they would include some reference to holding the line against change. Change is not only difficult, but also often seen as inherently evil or at least counterproductive. In general, comfort is derived from knowing what to expect in life.

The reaching-back, traditional congregation is characterized by a strong *appreciation for the stability created by well-worn, tried and true methods of doing things.* These congregations, which value responsibility and duty, often link those virtues to maintaining traditional practices and standards that have little to do with God's priorities. This desire for control and consistency tends to push some of these congregations to the point of imposing unnecessary rules and standards. It must be understood that the motive for much of this control is fear that a breakdown of standards and conduct will result in losing the important fundamentals of the faith or tradition.

Many of us grew up in reaching-back congregations. The church was much more than a place of worship and Christian fellowship. *It was the center of social life for the community.* We could find there a deep sense of identity in the social mosaic, if not in the kingdom of God. Oftentimes the pecking order of power in the secular community was lived out in the church. With all of the various social agendas playing on the same field, it is not difficult to see that the traditional congregation is perhaps the most difficult church to understand and define.

Examples

The Lutheran church in which I grew up provides one example of a reaching-back congregation. It plays a powerful and positive role in the lives of the families that made up the congregation in rural South Dakota. I can recall with warm memories the harvest festivals, Sunday school picnics, Christmas programs, and softball games (all of which constituted a major part of my early socialization). When asked to come back to speak at the centennial celebration of this congregation, I was struck by how little things had changed from forty years earlier when I was sitting in Mrs. Nelson's second grade Sunday school class. The order of the service was the same. People sat in the same places, in the same pews. Everyone was older of course; some of the people in leadership now were my former classmates, but they acted much the same way I remember their parents' acting. The two or three new families that I did not recognize were conspicuous in that they were the only part that did not look familiar. The building had the same smells, and the church bell rang just as it did four decades earlier. After the morning service the people conversed with the same clichés and offered the same polite greetings to one another. The discussions about how the children and the corn were growing and the commentaries on the news of the community and the nation reflected the same common-sense, midwestern conservatism that I remember so well as a child. Most of my basic values were shaped by the influence of this small traditional community, where the church was perhaps the most important point of reference.

Another example of the reaching-back church is seen in the Baptist congregation that I attended while a university student. The traditions in this congregation were different than those of my Lutheran upbringing, but the sociological dynamics looked familiar. People within the Baptist congregation had a more theological agenda in their conversations, and the social and moral expectations were more carefully laid out. For example, it was understood that Christians were to stay clear of the five deadly sins of drinking, smoking, movies, cards, and rock music. It was also understood that five great virtues were to be honored: attendance at all Sunday meetings (Sunday morning worship, Sunday school, and Sunday evening gatherings), participation in Wednesday prayer meetings, tithing, daily devotional Bible reading, and regular witnessing. My exposure to the Bible in this congregation was critical to my personal spiritual development and played a big role in my coming to personal faith.

Strengths

The strengths of the reaching-back church can be too easily overlooked by those who wear creativity as a badge of spiritual virtue. To overlook the strengths of these traditional churches is a big mistake.

1. Traditional congregations appreciate the security and stability created by resisting change. This power builds confidence and can have a significant influence in shaping the beliefs and behaviors of people. Many people believe that one of the most damaging characteristics of our modern age is its inability to sustain any kind of social, ethical, and relational constancy and momentum. Pluralism and individualism have become so sacred that notions of unity, conformity, and duty are not only viewed as outdated, but also threatening. Without traditions, we lose the stability we need to cope with the unavoidable changes that confront us. In a world where so much is changing, it is comforting to know that some things do not, or should not, change.

2. Most of what seems so innovative and relevant to the progressive congregation may be little more than a fad. As one person put it, "When it is all said and done, have we served our children well by familiarizing them with a few praise mantras while not introducing them to the classic hymns of the faith?" Praise songs like "Majesty, Worship His Majesty" that perhaps do not have the shelf life of "A Mighty Fortress Is Our God" may be fun in the short-term, but will they link one generation to another? Can we identify with the faith of our ancestors without also sharing some of the language and timeworn expressions of their faith?

3. Respecting the consensus of the whole body of Christ—both living and dead—is important. Someone has defined church tradition as giving a vote to those who have gone on before us and are now with Christ. If we are one body with many members that transcend time and space, does that not compel us to cherish with sensitivity the contributions of previous generations? This current generation's love affair with the present leaves some of us feeling insecure and superficial.

4. The sacrifices of those who have gone before and paid a price to build the present deserve respect. Many believers are aware that their ancestors paid a price for the building of the present establishment. It seems like an act of profound disrespect to overthrow or ignore what they have worked so hard to build. In a sense, the traditional congregation is often driven by a sentimental love for their spiritual ancestors. To change things is to violate memories and desecrate the grave sites of those who are deeply loved and fondly remembered. In one Baptist church, the idea of doing away with the Sunday evening evangelistic service was thwarted in spite of the fact that no non-Christian (and very few Christians) had attended in several years. The driving reason seemed to rest with the fact that two of the influential deacons had come to faith at that meeting some fifty years earlier, and its continuation was a memorial to their personal experience.

Concerns

1. Does the reaching-back church confuse creed and culture? To confuse the wine and the wineskin can be a problem for all of us, but this is especially a concern with the traditional, reaching-back church. It is not at all certain that the vision and faith of the reformers can be preserved by rigidly adopting the style and culture of the reformers. The content of Luther's catechism may be worth preserving, but the catechetical style of learning should be negotiable. Changing the hour of worship and the length of the service on Sunday does not mean that a church has lost its faith in the resurrection of Christ. It may mean that it is secure enough to be faithfully flexible in reaching a generation that will come to a Saturday night meeting and not a Sunday morning meeting. For some of the congregations in the community where I grew up, long-standing feuds over traditions seemed to have no bearing on basic Christian orthodoxy. For example, one congregation split over a change in the denominational hymnal. The debate was waged with theological vocabulary, but seemingly only for dramatic emphasis in that the people in the congregation were disinterested in theology up until the point of the hymnal change. The real threat was change of any type.

A conservative Baptist congregation in a small town in Iowa spent two years debating and fighting, before it split, over the use of a Bible translation other than the King James Version. We are not suggesting that there is not legitimate room for debate about preferred translations of the Bible, but in this case the debate was not on the serious merits of the majority Greek text (behind the King James Version) over against the critical Greek text (the basis of most modern translations). The debate was over change and tradition. To change the way things had been constituted a departure from the true faith in the minds of some of these people.

2. *Are these congregations more committed to conservatism than Christianity?* This failure to distinguish between classical and cultural conservatism is a common problem in many congregations. Classical conservatism consists of a world and life view that is shaped by biblical presuppositions, such as the beliefs that God exists and that God is not silent, the notion that we are morally accountable to love God and one another, the reality of the supernatural, and the unique inspiration of the Bible. Cultural conservatism, on the other hand, consists of a mind-set that is closed to change or reason and is committed to a political, social, economic, and stylistic tradition that is not open to review or change. It is bigoted, dogmatic, defiant, sectarian, defensive, and angry. It is critical of the present age, but uncritical of the previous age from which it derived its traditions. It needs to recognize that at one time the previous age was someone's present age. The tendency to be conservative with a capital "C" and Christian with a lowercase "c" is sometimes the pattern. The result is a proud and judgmental spirit based on human tradition and little else.

A young student from a Southern Baptist background approached me after one of my sermons and asked, "How do you expect anyone to get saved in this church without an altar call?" I reminded him that the altar call is a tradition growing out of early American revivalism. Although it is never mentioned in the Bible, it had become a sacred practice in his mind and unfortunately in the mind of many. I have nothing against an altar call in the proper setting, but it is a wineskin issue not a wine issue. It is a style issue not a fundamental issue of the faith.

Reaching-back churches can also become desensitized to the real issues of spiritual warfare while expending all the ammunition on battles that, in the end, mean little or nothing. How many congregations have allowed fellowship between believers to be broken over the preservation of an outdated tradition such as the style of a sermon or the preservation of a meeting?

3. Are these churches susceptible to legalism, that is, to expand the boundaries of orthodoxy beyond the revelation of Scripture? Do these congregations harshly judge others who do not hold to the same tradition that they embrace? Are they insensitive to the difference between what is major and what is minor, what is fundamental and what is negotiable? The traditional church is sometimes quick to critique modern cults for adding to the revelation of Scripture while it is uncritical of its own additions, such as cultural rules and mores.

The traditional church can become legalistic in that it judges people superficially for not holding to arbitrary traditions as though they were sacred. For example, in some congregations the use of wine is forbidden and anyone using wine would be barred from membership. Is this an issue that should divide Christians? In some traditional congregations the answer is a confident and loud *YES!* While this legalistic tendency is more often found in theologically conservative congregations, it is also present in congregations that do not have a conservative theological base, but are nonetheless culturally conservative. In the more liberal traditions it might be political or liturgical correctness that is the issue.

4. Can these congregations harden slowly into rigid and inflexible forms, whether of habit or of opinion? Is the traditional church a reaching-back church because it is not looking in any of the other directions—up, down, in, out, or forward? Is there any flexibility? Can needed changes take place without major trauma? Is there any room for creativity? Can faithfulness and flexibility coexist?

I am reminded of the statement of a visitor to a very traditional, liturgical, worship service. "If this service is a reflection of the character of God, then he must be very boring, out-of-touch, and tired." What a pathetic distortion of the living Christ! Now to be sure, the answer to a boring service is not found in a cosmetic face-lift via pop music and change for change's sake. Respect for tradition without reverencing it at the expense of relevance is important.

5. In trying to preserve the past, are these churches arbitrarily selective? For example, some congregations are very interested in preserving the schedule of a previous generation, but not its technology. Somehow we are convinced that if we do away with the Wednesday night family prayer meeting we are undermining the family more than by getting rid of the TV set. In some cases, to discontinue the Sunday night evangelistic service would be seen as losing a heart for souls while in fact it might just be a realization that this form is not working.

Many reaching-back congregations focus attention on the era of the formation of their distinct character. For some congregations, it is the era of the congregation's glory days (usually the first generation of its existence). Other congregations see their origin in the Protestant Reformation and try to preserve elements of the sixteenth century through music, learning styles (catechisms), and ministry agendas (fighting theological battles that are over). Still other congregations identify with early North American revivalism and preserve patterns such as the camp meeting and revival tent in honor of their point of origin. The point is: The traditional church, in trying to fight against the destructive encroachments of modern culture, could uncritically marry the culture of a former era or more accurately a romantic notion of that culture.

If we can leave one piece of advice with the reaching-back church it would be: Help the rest of us appropriately appreciate our heritage by showing us its power and value. Do not just ask us to blindly follow tradition, but help us to save the baby without the bath water. Put your best foot forward, but do not kick your neighbor or lose your balance.

THE REACHING-BACK CHURCH

Strengths
- Stability
- Resistance to fads
- Giving the past saints a vote
- Respect for those who have gone before

Concerns
- Confusing creed and culture
- More conservative than Christian
- Legalism
- Inflexibility
- Selective use of the past

Examine Yourself

1. If your church is a reaching-back congregation, how far back is it reaching? What are the origins of its traditions?
2. If your congregation is not reaching back, will it be a

generation from now? Are you presently creating "the good old days" for a future generation?

3. How have your traditions helped or hindered your ministry? Has the net effect been good or bad?

4. Do you agree with the assessments of this chapter? In what way? What would you add or subtract?

8.

THE REACHING-FORWARD (SOCIAL ACTION) CHURCH

AFFECTING OUR CULTURE AS WISE, ALIEN AMBASSADORS

Christianity that does not start with the individual, does not start. Christianity that ends with the individual, ends. Today a growing number of churches, from conservative to liberal, have come to see that the gospel message has implications that need to be pressed upon the entire cultural environment beyond the community of believers. These congregations are the looking-forward or reaching-forward churches that want to change the shape of the future of the whole society.

Ephesus

When Paul brought the gospel to ancient Ephesus, who could not have imagined the social turmoil that would result? The facts are recorded in Acts 19. The city of Ephesus, guardian of the temple of the pagan god Artemis, hosted a large industry of silver idol manufacturing. As the people of Ephesus were coming under the moral influence of the Spirit of Christ, they were turning from their old values, including the purchasing of these idols. The economic and cultural pressure brought by the church at Ephesus rose to the place that riots in the streets threatened the life of the apostle Paul. Here we have a clear first-century example of the gospel affecting the broader society as the values of God's kingdom controlled the socioeconomic lives of the believers.

This same phenomena has been observed throughout the history of the church from Constantine's Christian state to William Wilberforce's abolition of slave trade in England to Martin Luther King, Jr.'s Civil Rights movement. A number of congregations today are characterized by an acute sensitivity to the social power of the Christian message, and we address their ministry style in this chapter on the reaching-forward church.

Characteristics

The reaching-forward, politically active congregation is characterized by at least three things. First, it is *committed to a political agenda*. That is to say, it wants to shape public policy, official legislation, and social mores beyond the walls of the Christian community. In the incarnation of God's love in Christ, it sees a model for the church's ministry. The church is called to be salt and light to the world with a concern not just for people's souls, but also for their bodies and environments. It sees sin as not just an individual problem, but also an institutional or systemic problem as well. These congregations believe that, if the church is to be serious about confronting the forces of evil, it must be politically and socially active.

The second characteristic of the reaching-forward church is its tendency to be *politically polarized*. Its political bias is generally either liberal or conservative. It may not follow a particular party's platform, but it does represent a political ideology. One person put it this way, "A political conservative is one who favors more state control of social moral issues and less state control of economic issues. The political liberal is just the opposite, favoring less control of social issues and more control of economic issues."

The third characteristic of the reaching-forward, politically active church is that it sees the *church's role as prophetic and pastoral to the whole community*. The church is viewed as responsible for the soul of the state much as the prophets and priests of the Old Testament were responsible for the nation Israel. Some of the more conservative, reaching-forward congregations look at America as a special nation in a neo-covenant relationship with God, not unlike Israel in the Old Testament.

A fourth characteristic of the reaching-forward church is that *it takes much of its instruction from the Old Testament*. Social action in the context of the state is illustrated more clearly in the Old Testament than in the New. Liberation themes, often popular with these churches, find vivid illustration in Israel's Exodus experience.

Examples

The rise of the Moral Majority and the powerful role of telecommunication have pushed a number of conservative congregations into national prominence. Some of these congregations are politically active, evangelical churches. Liberty Baptist Church in Lynchburg, Virginia, and Coral Ridge Presbyterian Church in Fort Lauderdale, Florida, are among the more prominent examples of conservative, politically active congregations. It should be noted that both of these congregations are usually classified as outreach-oriented churches, but in recent years their focus seems to have shifted, at least in terms of the pulpit ministry. Neither of these congregations support a particular political party, but they both represent a definite political ideology that is identified as economically conservative, nationalistic, and Christian. These congregations see their political social agenda as a crusade to save American society from at least insignificance, and at worst, the judgment of God.

At the other end of the social action spectrum are the congregations that have a very different political bias. They are politically and sometimes theologically more progressive or liberal (note that the two ideologies are not always synonymous). In many cases it is more accurate to describe these congregations as critics of the present American status quo: the middle class. The Church of the Saviour in Washington, D.C., might fall into this category. The more liberal, socially active congregations are often smaller and less prominent than the conservative megachurches mentioned in chapter 8. The politically liberal congregations focus attention on the dark side of the American system; its racism, materialism, and economic exploitation of the weak by the powerful. They note God's concern for the oppressed and the poor, and they conclude that the church should show preference for the same through benevolent acts of charity and love. These congregations see their Christian crusade as not that of preserving, but of reforming what is, in their eyes, a fundamentally unjust and barbaric system. They tend to view alternative political models (often some form of socialism) as preferable to the present system.

Strengths

1. These congregations see the importance of the church breaking out of its holy huddle and making contact with the larger society. They expect the church to influence society in a positive way. They turn away from a strictly private faith or morality to affirm the need for a public, prophetic, and practical affirmation of kingdom values. They affirm the calling of the church to influence the world at all levels. If Christ is Lord, he is Lord of all and that includes the great institutions of society, such as government, education, entertainment, and the court system.

2. *These congregations see the power of systems and institutions as they shape the lives of individuals.* They know, for example, that education is a powerful influence in society, especially in the way history and ideals are presented. As someone put it, "He who controls the present, controls the future; and he who controls the past, controls the present." Political conservatives and liberals alike know that the way our history is portrayed will shape our future expectations and conduct. If, for example, our children are led to believe that America's history has been dominated by virtuous heroes of traditional values, then it is easier to expect that same traditional style to continue. If, on the other hand, America can be portrayed as a nation dominated by secular and materialistic values, then it is much easier to promote those same values today.

The reaching-forward congregations know that injustice and violence are institutional and that economic, legal, medical, and law enforcement systems must be addressed as part of an ongoing battle for truth, justice, and peace. Again, the battles often find conservative and liberal Christians on opposing sides fighting each other, but they agree on this one point—the institutional systems of democracy are worth fighting over.

3. *These churches accept the prophetic role that the church must take in a fallen world.* If the church and its members do not speak the truth of the gospel with clarity and sensitivity to the social needs of our day, who will? For evil to prosper we need only for people with the truth and love of God to remain silent.

4. *These congregations recognize that love requires action, not just preaching and praying.* They mobilize, march, write letters to their representatives in Congress, start projects, and so on. "As a society becomes more complex in its economic, social, and political dynamics, it requires more than a one-on-one

approach to ministry. The systems need to be challenged and changed." These were the words of a pastor who had left a traditional church for a more politically active congregation in Washington, D.C.

Concerns

1. Do these churches place too much stock in the political machinery of a society? When Jesus chose twelve disciples who were politically powerless and socially insignificant, what was he saying? When Paul noted that God had chosen the foolish and the weak to confound the wise and the strong (1 Cor. 1:27), what was he suggesting? Where is the real power in God's kingdom? Can the justice, peace, respect, and freedom that many Christians long for in society be secured through political force? What happens when Christians are put in positions of power in a secular society? Do things really change in the way they would expect or want?

2. Why do the apostles say so little about political involvement of the early church? It is interesting to note the way in which Jesus and the apostles address or ignore the social and political issues of their day. Almost all of their attention seems centered upon the infrastructure of the Christian community, that is, how Christians relate to one another. When issues are addressed, such as slavery in 1 Peter and Philemon, the posture is politically passive. What does this suggest to us? When we look into the Old Testament record, we find much of the same kind of restricted horizons in the application of social ethics. The infrastructure of the covenant community, in this case Israel, is the focus. Justice and freedom among the Canaanites and the Egyptians did not seem to be a major issue with God.

3. Do these churches give less attention to personal moral issues than to unjust political systems? While fighting the big Goliaths of society, a congregation can ignore the moral and emotional diseases of its own family. Some of the most powerful religious figures in American social change, when the biographers are honest, have led personal lives that were not only inconsistent with their position, but also apparently unchallenged by the church. Too often we see the real moral issues as political and too quickly see personal ethics as optional.

4. Do these churches accept society's definition of key terms such as justice, peace, love, and freedom? These are biblical words, but it is easy for both conservatives and liberals to allow American culture to define them. For example, is biblical peace primarily psychological, political, or spiritual? Does love mean giving people what they want (what they think will make them happy), or does it mean giving them what they need (what will make them holy)? Does justice mean democratic power, economic equality, and individual autonomy, or does it mean God's sovereign plan for each individual no matter how unfair their lot might appear? Does God have the right to define roles for individuals and nations, or are social roles to be based on individual achievement only? Does freedom mean that every individual has a right to make his or her own laws, define their own destiny, and go their own way; or does it mean that they are liberated to serve others and worship their Creator?

A big part of the political conflict within the church has to do with the way we define the terms that characterize God's kingdom. Another point of conflict has to do with the role of the King. Is God instrumental in the realization of his kingdom or simply a herald of it?

5. Can these churches be more in love with a vision of the kingdom than with the King? Sometimes we get the impression with both our more liberal and conservative friends that a passion for a particular vision of the kingdom is the single most important issue in their Christian faith. This passionate vision renders Jesus little more than a chaplain for the system, be it left or right of the political center. For example, the peace movement in many congregations seems to be committed to a certain view of political tranquility and justice with or without Christ as Lord. The fact that he is called the Prince of Peace puts him on "our side," but if he turned out not to share our political vision or to be politically incorrect, then we would ignore or resist him as we do all others who "haven't seen the light." When faced with biblical testimony that does not fit the image of the pacifist Jesus, we ignore or explain the texts away as cultural lint in the otherwise authoritative revelation. As one friend put it, "Without progressive political implications, theology is irrelevant."

Conservative congregations can be just as susceptible to this pitfall. How many believers experience some discomfort when the American flag is paraded to the tune of patriotic songs in a service of worship reserved for Christ as Lord? Even Israel, the only ordained theocracy, would have viewed as blasphemous some of the commingling of God and country in worship that is standard in some conservative, politically active congregations.

6. *Can political bias blind us to certain inconsistencies?* For example, are we selective in what we choose to see as moral issues? We cannot help recalling a pair of bumper stickers on a van in Chapel Hill, North Carolina. One sticker said, "Save the whales" while the other read "Vote Pro-Choice."

Politically conservative congregations are rightly concerned about the abortion epidemic, sexual permissiveness, and biased values in public education, but why do they not seem as concerned about competitive individualism, institutional racism, idolatrous nationalism, and consumptuous materialism? If conservatives have forgotten one thing, it is the doctrine of a sinful nature that infects not only liberals, but also conservatives. It may take more than getting conservative Christians in places of high office to bring peace and justice or even truth. We also need to remind ourselves that God's plan does not center on raising up a just and righteous America, but on building his church. God may use the decadence in America to strengthen his church. His ways are often mysterious and different from ours. But of this we can be sure: God is not as pro-American as some of us are.

Do politically liberal congregations have a better leg to stand on? Hardly. While they are rightly concerned about the issues of sexism, racism, and economic imperialism, why cannot they also see the moral tragedy of the growing vacuum of eternal values that exist in American culture? Are they not aware that their liberal political agenda seems to follow step for step (be it a few years late) with the agenda of the modern secular university that seems committed to defining reality and making decisions as though God does not exist? One person put it this way, "We can't be sure of the Scripture's teaching about the nature of the Godhead, but of this we can be certain: She is for the ordination of women and against capitalism." Can we be so sure, for example, that a socialistic political ideology is loving? It might seem the most compassionate response to the poor, but is it effective in reaching its ideals of justice, peace, and prosperity for all? It was Winston Churchill who reminded us that if a person is not a socialist by the time he is thirty-five, he needs his heart examined; and if he is still a socialist after thirty-five, he needs his head examined. Just as the conservative congregations look like chaplains of the status quo of a previous generation, the liberal congregations look like court jesters for the revolutionary idealists.

If we could leave a few words of advice to the reaching-forward congregations, it would be the following. Show us how to make a difference in our communities and nation without losing our perspective on the limits of political power and the priorities of the New Testament. Do not reject us if we differ with you politically. Do not judge us by our political stands more than by our spiritual character and heart. Do not lose patience with us when we ask questions that seem for the moment to slow down the process of social change. And do not let us ignore those outside the church who suffer physically. Put your best foot forward, but do not kick your neighbor or lose your balance.

THE REACHING-FORWARD CHURCH

Strengths
- Expect to influence society
- Respect the power of social systems
- Accept a prophetic role
- Put love in action

Concerns
- Too much faith in political power
- The silence of the early church
- Ignoring personal morality
- Letting society define key concepts
- Kingdom without the King
- Political bias

Examine Yourself

1. Is yours a forward-reaching, politically active congregation? In what sense is it or is it not? Do you feel that it is on the right track? How are you involved personally in the social, political agenda of your church?
2. What would an ideal society look like in your mind? How realistic is that vision? Will it be realized before Christ's return? In what sense?

3. What do you think of America? In what sense should Christians be supporting a representative democracy, a capitalistic economy, Judeo-Christian ethical values in a pluralistic state?
4. How do you assess Christian congregations that take a different sociopolitical stand than yours? Are these differences more divisive than they should be? How should the strong feelings be handled that some Christians have toward those who disagree with them?
5. Do you agree with the assessments of this chapter? In what way? What would you add or subtract?

9.

LESSONS FOR YOUR CHURCH

After reviewing the six styles of ministry in this book, a number of lessons follow that we believe can be helpful for your church.

1. Identify your strengths. Most congregations may not know where or if they fit any of the six styles described in this book. In fact, most congregations are a combination of several strengths, just as individuals have a combination of several gifts or talents. How can you identify the strengths and weaknesses of your church's style? How can you then constructively relate to the strengths and weaknesses?

A congregation can explore its identity and recognize its primary area of strength in three helpful ways. First, *church leaders can ask those who come to the church questions about why they come.* Every few months in our congregation we have a social event called a Newcomer's Welcome. Three of the questions we ask people as they introduce themselves are (1) Why did you first come to this church? (2) Why did you keep coming? (3) What do you like and dislike about what you have found here? We note that three areas of ministry are mentioned repeatedly—teaching, worship, and relationships. This information tells us a lot about what our strengths are. Also, when our elders visit the small groups in our church, they ask people for feedback with respect to what God is using in this church to minister to their lives. When and if this feedback reveals a common theme, it will be a significant clue as to what style of ministry the church represents.

Second, *look at the passions and gifts of the senior staff.* What are the strengths of the senior staff, especially that of the head pastor? Pastoral gifts may provide a strong indication of a congregation's strength, especially if they are consistent with the historical emphasis of the congregation. You might ask yourself which of the six styles is the strongest motivator among the senior staff in your church.

In some cases, a senior minister is trying to be or do something that is a part of the church's tradition, but not his gift. In such a case, the emphasis of the pastor's ministry may not be his strength. For example, we have had contact with a number of churches that were historically committed to outreach, but were frustrated in their effectiveness. They were much more effective in providing the security of long-standing traditions or in providing gracious fellowship because that was where the pastors were gifted. In such cases, it might be good for those congregations to accept that reality and not try to fight it.

Third, *look at where the growth is taking place.* People vote with their feet and pocketbook. If people do not show up for worship with some enthusiasm, worship is probably not one of the your church's strengths. If people are not excited about being sensitive and sacrificial in reaching out to others, do not conclude that your church is market-driven. In such a case, you may want to be a market-driven church, but you are probably not there yet.

What happens when the strength and passion of the pastor and of the congregation are at odds? For example, when you have a traditional (reaching-back) congregation with a young market-driven (reaching-out) pastor, this mismatch is almost always a problem unless some flexibility and patience exist on both sides.

A congregation would do well to be careful in calling a pastor who has a different style than that of the congregation.

2. *Major on your strengths while not ignoring weaknesses.* Play to your strengths, not your weaknesses. Major on what you do well. If your church does several things well, be thankful and keep it up, but remember that most congregations will have one primary area of strength.

In our fellowship, we recognize that many of the people who come to our congregation do so because of the teaching ministry in our church. We are also strong in two other of the six areas— reaching up and in. We are weaker in reaching out, forward, and back. For this reason we give the teaching, worship, and relational ministries greater, not lesser, emphasis. We accept these strengths as gifts to be spotlighted. If a football team has a great passing game, they would be foolish to keep it under wraps and emphasize the running game until it became as strong as its passing game. To be sure, some balance is needed in order for the overall ministry to operate, but we do not feel as though we must do everything equally well. For example, we do not feel guilty because we are not a market-driven church, nor do we feel uncomfortable because we are not as sensitive to some traditional aspects of worship and church polity. We also do not feel badly about ourselves because we are not as socially active as some other congregations.

But now we come to a very important point. We do not belittle or look down on congregations that are stronger in those areas where we are weak. We are very careful to respect those who differ from us in those areas and to encourage them openly and regularly. We recognize that we are vulnerable in the areas where we are weaker and, therefore, draw upon other congregations to help us.

Recently we invited Timothy Dudley-Smith, an Anglican bishop and hymn writer, to speak to our congregation about the rich tradition of hymnody in the history of the church. This area is one where we can learn from those who have different strengths from ours. He was well received by our people, and we sensed that he left us feeling personally encouraged by Christ's Spirit in our congregation, even though our church represented a very different style from his own tradition. Over the years we have tried to invite leaders from different styles of ministry to speak to us and broaden our appreciation for the whole body of Christ.

We have not hesitated to refer needy members in our congregation to other churches and ministries when we felt the individuals could be helped by them. On one occasion we had a pastoral problem that seemed beyond the scope of our wisdom or ministry. We referred this person to a pastor of a congregation that differed considerably from ours in emphasis. However, we knew that this man had a powerful prayer ministry in the area of this person's need. The results were dramatic and lifesaving for the person. We would not agree with some aspects of this neighbor's ministry, but we respected his strengths and knew him as a brother. In this case, his area of strength made a life-changing difference.

3. Encourage, do not ridicule, those congregations that have styles different from yours. It is too easy to hear a negative report about another church and feel just a little better knowing that is not your problem. Fight that fleshy insecurity and commit yourselves to give one another the benefit of the doubt on many issues. We must refuse to spread gossip about other ministries with styles that render them vulnerable where we are strong. We must be quick to offer genuine words of appreciation and respect to those around us. We vividly remember almost all of the times other pastors have paid compliments to our congregation. These compliments mean the most when they come from people who are furthest from our ministry emphasis and style. It means a lot to know that the Body of Christ does not wear a denominational or nondenominational label. When we stand before our

Maker, we will not be charismatics, Presbyterians, Baptists, Methodists, Anglicans, and so forth. We will be brothers and sisters. Let us start rehearsing for that day now.

4. Accept the fact that some people will not be attracted to your church's particular emphasis. Resist the temptation (1) to feel guilty if someone does not prefer the style of your church or (2) to look down on them for their poor judgment. It is important for your church to complement and coordinate with other ministries. The way your congregation relates to other congregations is a key indicator of the spiritual health of your posture as an individual congregation in the kingdom of God. One of the most embarrassing characteristics of the American church is its competitive spirit, in which congregations act as though they are competing for people, money, reputation, power, and recognition. This competition is blatantly inconsistent with the Spirit of Christ, but perfectly consistent with the spirit of our carnal culture. In short, do not compete with other congregations.

You might say, "But many of them don't do things the way we think they should be done." No doubt, but is that a reason to maintain an independent spirit? If we were consistent in demanding complete agreement before we cooperated, most of us would live and die in isolation.

Now to be sure, we are all well advised to protect and insist on fundamentals in our fellowship. However, the threat is that every matter of style and taste gets elevated to the status of a fundamental. Some of us grew up in a denomination where we could not take communion with those outside our synod or association even though our doctrinal beliefs were virtually identical. The only real difference seemed to be our European ancestry—one group was Scandinavian and the other was German.

Do not be afraid to say to other congregations, "We need your help in this area" or "some of our people need to become a part of your ministry because they need what you offer." I suspect that these words are seldom spoken, and it is shocking and sad that they are not. We need to learn that our credibility with the whole Christian community increases as we acknowledge what others probably already know, that we have weaknesses. We cannot do everything as well as we probably think we can or would like to do.

One of the ways in which we have tried to apply this awareness in our own congregation is through the tangible help we try to give to new churches in the community. We are an independent, nondenominational church, but we are not anti-denominational. When the PCA (Presbyterian Church in America) targeted our area for a new church, we invited the founding pastor to take our pulpit at all three Sunday morning services. We introduced him and his work and encouraged those worshiping with us who were looking for a more reformed emphasis in ministry to pray about joining in the planting of this new church. We had about fifty people respond by leaving us to join the PCA congregation. We knew how hard it is to start a congregation from scratch, and we wanted to give this new group as much encouragement as we could. We have extended the same sort of helping hand to several other churches from various traditions differing from our own emphasis. One was Wesleyan Methodist, another charismatic, and another Baptist. The members that left us were quickly replaced by newcomers, and the spirit of unity established with these new congregations has lasted for years. We all benefited from the effort.

5. Respect the need for a certain amount of balance in your church. A congregation is not exempt from functioning in all six areas—reaching up, down, in, out, back, and forward. An analogy can be drawn from the teaching of the apostle Paul in 1 Corinthians 12. Each believer had a gift or gifts for service. No one person had all the gifts. We need one another's strengths. This does not mean that any of us are exempt from obedient service in areas where we may not be gifted. For example, your gift may not be faith, but you are still expected to trust God. Your gift may not be administration, but you are still expected to order your life. Your gift may not be teaching, yet we are all to admonish and teach one another (Col. 3:16). In the same way, for example, a church may not be worship-centered, but it is still expected to offer a worshipful service.

Every church needs to use all the ministry styles to some degree in order to maximize its strengths. For example, a reaching-up or worship-centered congregation needs teaching and relationships to be effective lest the worship be hypocritical or misplaced. The teaching-centered church needs relationships, worship, tradition, social action, and outreach lest the teaching fall short of its goal to encourage integration of faith into all of life.

6. *Expect God to use you just the way you are.* One of the common fantasies of the American evangelical church is the notion that its weaknesses and failures will disqualify it from fruitfulness. In spite of the fact that the biblical record is filled with stories to the contrary, we still are intimidated by our insufficiencies and failures. The accuser of the brethren has no trouble reminding us of the areas where we are weak. On the other hand, if we should be so blessed as to have very few weaknesses, Satan loves to dull our memories of the ones we do have. After all, pride is just as effective as guilt in getting us to do things his way.

7. *Learn to appreciate and support your congregation's style even when it is not your personal preference.* Many congregations suffer unnecessary stress because someone in the congregation starts a personal crusade to change the church to match their personal style preference. For example, sometimes individuals with a longing for, let's say, charismatic worship or social action, feel so strongly about the absolute necessity of their preference that they lose their focus on what God is doing in their church. It is possible to be so concerned about what God is not

doing that we overlook and miss what he is doing. Just remember: God does not have to, and probably will not do it all through your congregation. Your individual style preference may be a legitimate part of God's plan for his church, but it is not the only style that God is concerned about. God is bigger than one style.

REFLECTIONS AND CONCERNS ABOUT THIS BOOK

The thesis of this book can be reduced to the following proposition. *Diversity of style among congregations should be seen as a call to mutual respect and support rather than a threat to unity.* We are not saying that all diversity is good, but where the differences are matters of style in ministry, let there be tolerance, appreciation, and mutual respect. We have tried to show some of the basic ways in which healthy Christian congregations differ in style. We have introduced a style sphere that encompasses six basic aspects of the church's calling. We have also tried to point out the strengths and concerns that accompany each style. Our greatest fear is that those who embrace one style might see their style as the only Christian way and overtly or covertly impose their style on all other congregations. This sort of forced uniformity would have the practical effect of dividing Christ's church by pitting one congregation against another. As Paul says of differences among individual believers, "If all were a single member, where would the body be? As it is, there are many members, yet one body" (1 Cor. 12:19-20). We believe that these words can be helpful for congregations as well.

We can summarize some of what has been said in this book with the following chart.

ACTS 2	STYLES OF CHURCH MINISTRY	LONGINGS OF MODERN PERSONS	PURPOSES OF CHRIST'S CHURCH	NEW TESTAMENT ILLUSTRAT-IONS
V. 43 *"A sense of awe"*	REACHING **UP**	**TRANSCEN-DENCE** (Worship) in the face of "technology"	**EXALT** Christ as Creator, Redeemer, Lord	**CORINTH**
V. 42 *"the teaching of the Apostles"*	REACHING **DOWN**	**INSIGHT** (teaching) in the face of "information"	**EDUCATE** Christ's people	**BEREA**
V. 42 *"fellowship"*	REACHING **IN**	**INTIMACY** (relationships) in the face of "isolation"	**EDIFY** Christ's church	**JERUSALEM**
V. 47 *"adding to their number daily"*	REACHING **OUT**	**DIRECTION** (tradition) in the face of "professionalism"	**EVANGELIZE** Christ's world	**ATHENS**
V. 42 *"breaking of bread"*	REACHING **BACK**	**STABILITY** (tradition) in the face of "temporality"	**ENCOMPASS** the past	**GALATIA**
V. 47 *"having favor with all the people"*	REACHING **FOR-WARD**	**UTOPIA** (ideal society) in the face of "injustice"	**ENRICH** the culture	**EPHESUS**

There are three possible objections to the material in this book that we would like to acknowledge and address.

Isn't "Style" Too Subjective?

The first objection is that the issue of style is not a useful way to distinguish between Christian congregations because it is too subjective. Many congregations simply cannot identify with only one of the six styles portrayed in this book. In contrast, the traditional ways of distinguishing between congregations by denomination, liberal/conservative, charismatic/non-charismatic, size, and so on is quite clear.

Our response would be threefold. First, if the issue of styles is ambiguous, each of the traditional ways of distinguishing between congregations is also subject to ambiguity. For example, some congregations such as Saddleback Community Church in southern California are technically denominational (in this case Southern Baptist), but look and act as though they are nondenominational. And when is a church conservative? How conservative does it have to be before that label is meaningful? What constitutes a charismatic church? When is a church large? A congregation of two hundred in rural Montana may be huge, while a congregation of the same size in the suburbs of Chicago or Los Angeles might be considered small. Any categorization is going to have ambiguity.

The second response we would make to the objection that style is too subjective a way to distinguish between congregations is that Scripture seems to distinguish between congregations either by orthodoxy (those that are true to the gospel or not) or by style (noted for outreach, community, worship, and so forth). It should be noted that neither distinction offers categories that are hard and fast.

The third response we would offer is that the six styles mentioned are not intended to be exhaustive. Each of the six styles could be broken down into substyles. For example, many varieties of worship-centered congregations exist. The same is true of reaching-out congregations.

Shouldn't Balance Be the Goal?

The second criticism that can be made of the thesis of this book is that a healthy church should strive to be strong and balanced in each of the six styles mentioned and should not have just one outstanding strength. We agree. It is certainly ideal and a blessing to be strong in every style, but we have observed that in fact most churches are not so blessed. An analogy can be made with respect to the individual believer. Every Christian is called to be conformed to the fullness of Christ, but this does not mean that every believer will have all the gifts that are in Christ. Paul was spiritually mature, and yet called to minister more specifically to the Gentiles (rather than the Jews). Furthermore, his role was more specifically that of spiritual "planting" (rather than watering). To be sure, Paul ministered also to Jews and did a lot of spiritual watering, but these activities were not his primary calling and probably not his long and strong suit. A church can be mature and yet have some areas of relative strength with respect to one style as compared to other styles.

Isn't Doctrine the Most Important Issue?

The third objection that might be raised is the fact that we give so little attention to doctrine in our discussion of style. Some might read this book and wonder if the only thing that really counts is style. No matter how far afield a congregation might be with respect to sound Christian theology, as long as they are successful at what they do, is it O.K.? Are we not guilty of the very thing we criticize, that being the adaptation of our culture's functional view of God where substance is replaced by style, theology by technique, and what is true by what works?

First, we want to say that orthodox doctrine is very important. However, many shades of gray are present in the spectrum of doctrinal orthodoxy. Rather than trying to distinguish every shade of gray along the way, we have chosen to take as generous a stand as possible with respect to judging congregations on their adherence to what we see to be the pure truth of the gospel. When we use the words *liberal* and *conservative,* we are generally referring to the range of diversity within that part of the church that holds to the most basic fundamentals of the faith—the special inspiration and authority of Scripture, the deity of Christ, the substitutionary nature of the atonement, the exclusive nature of salvation by faith in Christ apart from human merit. This list could be shorter or longer, but it gives the reader an idea of what we consider fundamental for the purpose of the discussion in this book. We realize that there will be no end to the discussion of what constitutes liberal and conservative and what is fundamental and what is not. That discussion is important, but not for the thesis of this book.

Unity with Diversity Is a Christian Distinctive

In the twenty-fifth chapter of Matthew, the parable of the talents teaches us that we are to be wise and not foolish with respect to the gifts God has given us. The parable indicates that each of us will be given different resources and will be accountable for how we use them. If we give attention to them so that they are multiplied for the benefit of the master's purposes, we will be a blessing to the master; and if we selfishly sit on them or use them to belittle others, we will be a disappointment to the master. We are not asked to be someone we are not, but we are expected to take risks in creatively using what we have been given in keeping with the master's purpose. This use of our gift will require that we take risks of faith and that we bear fruit from the strengths that are given us while respecting others with different strengths. This book has been concerned with applying the principle of stewardship to gifts, given on the congregational level. In our view, a healthy successful congregation is one that is competent in each of the six areas of ministry highlighted in the style sphere, and it will be outstanding in at least one of those areas.

We might use the analogy of a basketball team. Someone must occupy each of the five positions on the team. A team will never be strong unless it is effective at each position, but everyone does not need to be the star. If you have a star, use that person—give him or her the ball often and do not apologize for the fact that he or she scores most of the points. And do not apologize when your church's strength attracts most of the newcomers. A congregation should be able to accommodate a wide variety of people, but it is true—some people will be more comfortable with one congregation than another because of differences in style of ministry.

Our passion is twofold. First, to bring unity to the body of Christ while preserving legitimate diversity in style among Christian congregations. Second, our passion is to effectively help build congregations that reach out, in, up, down, back, and forward. While realizing that our church will always reach in some of those directions better than we will in others, we want to accept the way God has made us without guilt for what we are not or pride for what we are. With what we learned on our sabbatical, we feel better equipped to make a significant contribution toward those ends in our own congregation. Our prayer is that this book will encourage other churches to those same ends.

Put your best foot forward, but do not kick your neighbor or lose your balance.

APPENDIX

DIAGNOSTIC QUESTIONS: TO MINISTER FROM YOUR STRENGTH

Any attempt at classification of a congregation's style is less than precise. Most congregations do not fall perfectly into one category. To help the reader we offer a number of questions that may be of assistance in applying the information presented in this book to a particular congregation.

The Six Styles

Prioritize each of the six styles as you respond to the following questions. Do this by assigning a numerical value (6 = highest or strongest to 1 = lowest or least) to each of the six styles in response to the following questions. By being forced to prioritize the six styles we are asking you to make some difficult choices. In some cases it may be easier to identify #6 (strongest) and #1 (weakest) first before numbering the rest. When you add the numbers to see which characteristics are preferred in your congregation you might have a hint as to your style, or preferences. If more than one person tries the evaluation, you will find inconsistencies that point to subjects that need work.

1. What are the most frequently praised aspects of your congregation's ministry? (Worship __, Teaching __, Relationships __, Outreach __, Social impact __, Tradition __)

2. What are the passions of the senior staff? (Worship __, Teaching __, Relationships __, Outreach __, Social impact __, Tradition __)

3. What was the strength of the founding (or previous) pastor(s)? (Worship __, Teaching __, Relationships __, Outreach __, Social impact __, Tradition __)

4. What draws you to this congregation? (Worship __, Teaching __, Relationships __, Outreach __, Social impact __, Tradition __)

5. Where do you feel your congregation has the most to offer other congregations in your community? (Worship __, Teaching __, Relationships __, Outreach __, Social impact __, Tradition __)

Add the numbers assigned to each of the six styles to identify its strength to your congregation: (Worship __, Teaching __, Relationships __, Outreach __, Social impact __, Tradition __)

Four Temperament Substyles

Each of the six styles can be further distinguished by the four classic temperaments. Respond to the following questions by assigning to each temperament a number (4 = most applicable to 1 = least applicable). Again, arrange or prioritize each of the four choices after each question.

1. What most characterizes your congregation's style? (law and order-SJ __, freedom and flexibility-SP __, philosophical and logical-NT __, warm and idealistic-NF __)

2. What does your congregation value most in facing personal problems? (moral rules and traditional regulations-SJ __, flexible and sometimes inconsistent methods-SP __, impersonal adherence to principles of truth-NT __, warmth and preservation of harmony-NF __)

3. What do people say is your congregation's greatest weakness? (too legalistic and rigid-SJ __, too disorganized and changeable-SP __, too philosophical and impersonal-NT __, too afraid of hurting someone's feelings-NF __)

4. What do people say is your congregation's greatest strength? (we have clear goals, answers, and standards-SJ __, we are adaptable and action oriented-SP __, we have a deep understanding of life and the Kingdom of God-NT __, we are warm and empathetic-NF __)

5. What is the most important aspect of spiritual maturity as understood by your congregation? (duty and discipline before the laws of God-SJ __, freedom to act in faith by the individual leading of the Spirit-SP __, adherence to the big picture of God's Kingdom-NT __, personal love and inclusion of others-NF __)

Now add up the numbers ascribed to each of the four temperaments. Which if any is dominant? (law and order oriented-SJ __, action oriented-SP __, truth oriented-NT __, caring oriented-NF __)

Faithful, Flexibly Faithful, or Flexible

To understand how your congregation is related to its theological confession and its temporal culture prioritize each of the following sets of options in response to each question below. Do this by assigning values (3 = very true of us, 2 = not clearly true of us, 1 = not true of us at all) to each set of options.

1. Our congregation (pastors) speaks to issues using the vocabulary of: (a) the Bible with little reference to cultural slang or popular terminology __, (b) biblical principles phrased in popular vocabulary, (c) the culture with little reference to biblical terms __

2. Our congregation spends most of its time trying to understand: (a) the text of the Bible with little reference to the issues of modern culture __, (b) biblical principles as they apply to the issues of our culture __, (c) the culture with little reference to biblical texts __

3. Our congregation understands its task as primarily: (a) teaching the Bible with little reference to changing cultural issues __, (b) articulating and applying biblical principles to current felt needs __, (c) addressing the needs of our culture with less reference to preaching the Bible __

4. Our congregation (pastor) sees the greatest threat to the church as: (a) the adapting of the world's agenda in ministry __, (b) an insensitivity to the application of the Scripture to modern life __, (c) the irrelevance of outdated "biblical" traditions when facing modern life __

5. Our congregation (pastor) sees the greatest strength of our church as its: (a) strong adherence to the traditional orthodox gospel __, (b) sensitivity to addressing modern issues with Christian insight __, (c) involvement in the trauma and ambiguity of modern life __

6. We: (a) have biblical answers to every question that is worth asking __, (b) have many issues where we must confess we just don't know the answer __, (c) we are certain of very little __

7. We: (a) have little respect for modern science (psychology, sociology, anthropology, and so on) __, (b) have a guarded respect for modern learning __, (c) rely upon modern learning as the most trustworthy source of understanding the Bible and reality __

8. We: (a) believe that if a person believes that the Bible is the inspired word of God, they will know the truth with certainty __, (b) believe that the Bible is authoritative but sometimes difficult to understand with complete certainty __, (c) believe that the Bible is nearly impossible to understand with any certainty __

Now add up the numbers assigned to (a) __ faithful, (b) __ flexibly faithful, (c) __ flexible. This may give you some idea of where your congregation fits. If more than one person ranked your style, you can work to express why you see different strengths and weaknesses.